GLYNDEBOURNE
PICNICS

Michael Smith's

GLYNDEBOURNE PICNICS

Foreword by Sir John Pritchard
Illustrations by Polly Raynes

Lennard Publishing
1989

Lennard Publishing
a division of Lennard Books Ltd
Musterlin House, Jordan Hill Road. Oxford OX2 8DP

British Library Cataloguing in Publication Data
Smith, Michael, 1921-
Michael Smith's Glyndebourne Picnics
1. Great Britain. Picnicking – Manuals
I. Title
642.3

ISBN 1 85291 039 9

First published 1989

Editor Michael Leitch

Additional material by Victoria Dickie

Design by Pocknell & Co

Typesetting by Goodfellow & Egan

Reproduced, printed and bound in Great Britain by
Butler and Tanner Limited, Frome

CONTENTS

FOREWORD

During the happy years I spent at Glyndebourne as Music Director I was often quizzed by foreign visitors on what they describe as the 'mystique' of a visit to the famous Sussex opera house: the whole business of interrupting their afternoon schedule in London, climbing into evening dress and (a little self-consciously) presenting themselves at the Glyndebourne train in crowded Victoria Station was rather daunting. An hour in the train could be devoted to a hurried brush-up on the libretto of 'L'Incoronazione di Poppea' or, even more exotically, Gershwin's 'Porgy & Bess': then a quick skirmish in the bus through Sussex lanes before the first glimpse of the Christie's House – somewhat sleepily preparing itself yet again for the daily invasion by a public intent on elegant pursuit of Culture. This particular travel method rarely permitted more than a snatched cup of tea or just possibly a magical Pimm's Cup, before the overture began: it remained for the civilised length of the main Interval to allow of a refined repast, prepared that morning and conveyed in picnic baskets carefully bestowed in selected spots of the beautiful gardens, to be savoured and hopefully to engender a dreamy contentment ideal for the second Act of the opera.

Of course, more experienced patrons who had been encouraged by favourable weather prospects often left town earlier, in order to stroll through the grounds without pressure and to partake of Afternoon Tea – I am delighted that Michael Smith's book will provide suggestions for this very English eventuality. Arrival in mid-afternoon not only gave country residents in the region of Haywards Heath somewhat alarming glimpses of stationary cars with gentlemen attempting to don evening trousers in the driving seat – there was also the distinct bonus of surprising famous opera singers engaged in rehearsing the operas clad *en deshabille* in a manner reflecting their temperaments: I remember a Yugoslav baritone who had somewhat unwisely affected a tartan kilt only to become the object of mirth from several 'exquisites', haughtily arriving for the Opera in an open Bentley.

This is all 'very Glyndebourne' and it is a feature of this amusing and invaluable book that the affectionate eyes of Michael Smith knowingly search out the occasionally bizarre requirements of patrons, whose varied approach to the art of opera finds a common ground in a determination to consume a good deal of food and drink. There should have been (perhaps there was) a cartoon showing The Man Who Took Fish Paste Sandwiches to a Glyndebourne

Picnic: and over the years there has I fancy developed a certain gently competitive spirit among the *cognoscenti* of the *al fresco* repast. I remember the slightly supercilious attitude adopted by the inner elite at Glyndebourne towards a gentleman who dined in style under one of the great trees shading the lake. While he relaxed at ease enjoying the first half of 'Figaro', his butler and chauffeur would transport the required antique table, festooned with white linen and silver, ice buckets, finest crystal, and the like. Then the gentleman, always alone, would take his place and enjoy a dinner warmed on a silver chafing-dish and served impeccably by his staff. This ostentation was thought to be exaggerated, only the impressively crested silverware preventing the possible accusation of vulgarity.

As a regular performer at Glyndebourne and its Music Director, I enjoyed an office and terrace, level with the rounded upper windows of the Organ Room. There the preparation and consuming of many Interval Suppers sometimes endangered, I'm afraid, the peaceful period of reflection a conductor should enjoy before continuing his interpretation. I was lucky in having, at my Sussex home, a convivial housekeeper (Mrs Mills) who took seriously the business of catering for my guests, and she worked her way through a variety of menus in the course of the Season, scarcely ever repeating herself. She was, however, particularly proud of her Boeuf Wellington and one day, anticipating a large number of guests, she produced a construction *en coûte* of truly massive proportions, seductively browned in the oven and festively adorned with my initials in pastry. Everyone pronounced it delicious, but following two lady guests down the stairs from my room I caught a telling comment, 'What did you think of that giant Sausage Roll?'

Before the Glyndebourne Picnic achieved the culinary heights celebrated in this book, I remember conducting the first part of Strauss' 'Ariadne', with the unforgettable Sena Jurinac as the composer. A friend of mine used the forty minutes of the Prologue to prepare, just backstage in the Conductors' Room, a tasty Canard à l'Orange over a portable electric stove. As the wonderful Composer–Zerbinetta duet was reached, I began to sense a succulence in the air, and I felt I knew whence it came. Looking up I noticed Sena, who loves her food, sniffing the air; by the time the curtain fell, several patrons in the front row were doing the same thing. Later I was told that Sena Jurinac, most unusually, had sent urgently to the restaurant at the interval demanding an immediate grilled steak. After this, we thought it more prudent to serve only cold food in the precincts of the stage . . .

Michael Smith over many years has shown his devotion to the arts of the opera *and* the kitchen. I know from experience that he has the true spontaneity of the great chef in using alternative ingredients when the desired ones are not at hand: and the lightness and humour of his regard for opera singers and their craft accords well with his insistence on *leggierezza* in cuisine. His association in this book with Victoria Dickie, an imaginative and innovative hostess, ensures that everyone of us will for the future take the institution of the Picnic with a proper respect and attention.

Sir John Pritchard

FIRST SIGHTINGS

I first went to Glyndebourne in 1955 and have been a regular visitor ever since, watching it change and grow from the very memorable day when I stopped dreaming about what it would be like and saw it for myself.

Whilst I had heard and read a little about the festival soon after returning from my training sojourns on the Continent, I had seen no *visual* reference to it. The words I had read – 'a small theatre in a Sussex hayfield', attached to some country mansion or other – conjured up a series of images: of a Palladian house, for example, and surely the theatre would be baroque, as at Chatsworth, or the house would be a *château* on the scale of Versailles, or perhaps it was like some *Schloss* on the Rhein . . . and if it were none of these, then perhaps it would be more in the style of Burlington's Assembly Rooms at York – all with their musical associations.

Mozart was performed at Glyndebourne – only Mozart – and all the very best singers from abroad were invited to appear. The sets were by Oliver Messel and . . . and I had also read that Glyndebourne had the most sophisticated lighting system in Europe, and therefore, at that time, in the world. Among my musical pals, all of whom I'd met up in my home county of Yorkshire, were John Pritchard and Geoffrey Parsons, who were involved in the music-making at Glyndebourne, and John Cox who was at the beginning of his career as a producer, working as assistant to Gunther Rennert. Yet it had never occurred to any of them to prepare me for the shock of the first sight of Glyndebourne: a concrete barn with iron arms for light fittings; no red plush, no gilt, no silk shades, and no crystal drops there, and the curtain was a dull sage green.

I knew and understood nothing of the unseen luxuries, the extensive rehearsal times for the artists and the dry (or wet!) acoustics. I still don't know as much as I'd like to about these things. I do know however that I love the sound opera makes and I shall never tire of it.

I found it most intriguing to dine in the concrete and plaster-walled dining halls with their wooden floors and vast trees growing up through the roofs, with the crisply starched tablecloths but still those stark wrought-iron lights. Oddly, the incongruous English names of the halls – Middle, Upper and Nether Wallop – were familiar to me for a sad reason; my eldest brother had been killed at Middle Wallop six weeks after the Second World War broke out.

My wife and I were guests of Anthony and Val Goldthorp, who were hosts of the very best sort. Observing what their guests enjoyed down to the subtlest of details was of paramount importance to them. 'I noticed your enigmatic smile when you tasted the *Auslesen*, so I thought you might well enjoy the *Beerenauslesen*.'

They, too, do not enjoy squatting when they eat (see 'The Stand-up Picnic'), though many of course do. Dishes and wines were ordered months in advance, as is still the way of things at Glyndebourne. There did, however, in those far off days, appear to be time to stroll through the gardens after eating, yet a glance through my early programmes tells me that seventy-five minutes was the allotted interval time then, as now. Maybe the service is slower or is it that the restaurants are busier?

I secretly wanted to essay a picnic – foie gras, lobster, game pie – very traditional stuff, you understand, but this wasn't to happen for some years, in fact not until we were first invited to hear 'La Pietra del Paragone' in the 1960s by John Pritchard. Even then, if my wife was with me, John would always entertain us in the Wallops. Eventually his picnics – which, in fact, were *grands soupers froids* – were served at table in the conductors' room, though somehow none of the spirit of the alfresco affair was lost, for there was always much to-ing and fro-ing and passing of dishes and pouring of champagne, served in those days in flat 'Marie Antoinette' saucers, until I introduced to the scene the first semi-flute and later the tall, elegant, paper-thin flutes from Baccarat.

As the years have rolled by, eating habits have changed in many and varied ways.

Operagoers are more sophisticated, not just in their musical knowledge ('Her voice is too big, don't you think?' 'She'll make a better Octavian . . .' and more folk tolerate or even actually like Henze, Weil and Knussen) but also in their enjoyment of food.

Gone are the heady days of caviar and foie gras with Roederer *Cristal*. Today people are more adventurous (or is it restless?), having been exposed to all aspects of wining and dining. Ethnic food is almost *de rigueur*, lighter eating is here to stay, theme picnics are popular and English food is enjoying a renaissance. That said, a quick glance at the contents of the unpacked hampers reveals that the 'cop-out' is still fairly popular, where platters piled with slivers of smoked salmon are passed around along with plates of brown bread-and-butter; and, as ever, strawberries or raspberries with thick cream still make a favourite finish to a picnic. And why not? For many the music has priority, and time to prepare elaborate dishes is at a premium.

That aside, this book is for those who are seeking to perfect the art of picnicking; for those who enjoy cooking and for those who take pride in attending to detail in order to give maximum pleasure to their guests.

EATING AT GLYNDEBOURNE: A SHORT HISTORY

The British love picnics and whenever they find an excuse during the summer to eat out of doors they will do so despite the dubious climate and general discomforts involved. The Glyndebourne audience is no exception to this curious rule of defiant optimism and it took the early visitors to the opera little time to discover that they had the perfect conditions (a long dinner interval and beautiful extensive gardens) to indulge this risky though oddly endearing passion. Yet it is an understandable one for on the evenings when the warmth of the daytime sun lingers and the still air smells sweet with roses and honeysuckle, there can be few pleasures to compare with the romance of eating an elegant and delicious picnic by the Glyndebourne lakes with the exquisite anticipation of the second half of a Mozart opera still to come.

It is difficult to pinpoint exactly when the Glyndebourne audience began to picnic in the interval. Earliest visitors to the Festival, when questioned, now say vaguely they never remember a time when people did not picnic. The first indication in the press that they were the norm was not found until 1951 when a photograph appeared in *The Sphere* of two young men sitting on a rug by the lake with a *fiasco* of chianti and a small rather shabby-looking suitcase (presumably housing the picnic) between them. In the earliest years of the Festival the whole audience, which then numbered 300, were catered for in the dining room. In 1936, £11 secured a subscription ticket for five performances including dinner which then cost 10s 6d. All the reports of the opening season mention the excellent dinner served between the acts. There are photographs in those early years of members of the audience wandering round the grounds with glasses in their hands but no indication that they are eating outside, and even in the beautiful Cartier-Bresson photos of the audience there is not a hamper or rug to be seen on the lawns.

Presumably a combination of the irresistible conditions for the romantic picnicker and larger audiences (the theatre was enlarged in 1952–53 to hold 718 seats) led to more people picnicking rather than using the restaurant so that in the last twenty years more than two-thirds of the audience on any given performance night eat their dinner outside. In 1983 the new Catering Management introduced a highly popular self-service restaurant – booking for which may be done up to the day of the performance thereby doing away with the strange system of deciding in February whether you want to eat lobster bisque or melon in July. Thanks to this, and possibly also to the increase in business sponsors and their parties, most of whom dine in one of the formal restaurants, the number of picnickers is actually falling and the restaurants are reclaiming their percentage.

Ideally the weather will be beautiful, quiet and balmy and the numerous groups of picnickers will be dotted around the lake, down by the ha-ha where the evening sun lingers longest, under the mulberry tree, by the white or blue borders or in the walled garden. The ideal place to picnic is very much up to the individual and people go to great lengths to make sure they get their favourite spot on each visit. The small round garden at the top of the lake is much favoured and is consequently often hideously overcrowded, presumably by people who all consider they have proprietorial rights to the place.

The *cognoscenti* will arrive early and lay claim to their particular patch with baskets, rugs, boxes and bottles. This practice has been known to misfire. One particular practical joker (now a well-respected member of the company) had a field day swapping round the neat piles of picnic equipment during the first act then hid in the bushes to enjoy the chaos at the beginning of the interval.

The style of picnics has changed considerably over the years. In the early days a picnic at Glyndebourne was largely like a picnic anywhere else (although as Bernard Levin pointed out in his article in the 1976 Programme Book, many will consider it heresy, if not indeed blasphemy, to say such a thing). The majority were content to sit on rugs, or cushions, the gentlemen particularly doing their best to reconcile the pleasure of doing justice to the salmon and champagne whilst sitting on the ground in evening dress. Nowadays more than half the picnickers bring chairs and tables and many go to great lengths to provide the most elegant of presentations for their picnics. Beautiful linen tablecloths, matching napkins, candelabra and little bowls of flowers for the table centre are not uncommon and at four o'clock in the afternoon the incongruous sight of elegantly dressed couples will be seen around the gardens, she laying the table with the very best china and silver while he decants some very fine wine into a claret jug in order to let it 'breathe' during the first act.

The ploy of tying string to your bottle of white wine and sinking it in the lake during the first act to keep cool is still used though never by this author. It must be a complicated procedure – if you can't find a bush with a small trunk near enough to the water, then your equipment must include a wooden stake and a hammer or an extremely large ball of string. The whole enterprise seems to depend on romance rather than practicality for its continued existence, but is none the poorer for that.

Some parties of course will have a butler to set their picnic up for them, either brought with them from home or rented in a package with the Rolls Royce and the picnic. The butler will double as chauffeur. Such parties will either have a first bottle of champagne or afternoon tea on arrival and will be able to walk around the grounds at leisure. None of the complicated business of setting up a three-course dinner for six and discovering what has been left behind – the chauffeur/butler will do it all during the first act.

But what happens if it is raining? An eventuality that has to be faced even by the optimists although the Glyndebourne administration is often blamed for meteorological disappointment as if it had engaged the wrong director. The answer before 1976 was to sit in the covered way, huddled under rugs, oilskins, fur coats and sou'westers stoically tucking into the picnic as if the sun were shining. Other options were Mildmay Hall (with its marquee-like drapes making it look like an Act II set for 'Albert Herring') which serves teas in the afternoon and has some tables and chairs, or the car. In 1976 John Player came to the rescue of the beleaguered picnicker and paid for the erection of a splendid marquee by the car park complete with pine tables and benches which now, on really miserable evenings, can squeeze in more than 200 people and their picnics. Rex Rogers, as master of ceremonies, is in charge. He sees to it that the candles in the bottles, provided by him for extra atmosphere, are lit; he coerces reluctant twosomes to share their table with others (often resulting in lasting friendships) and performs miracles with the floor space to fit in as many outcasts from the rain and wind as possible. The result is a warm and very convivial party atmosphere and the initiated will arrive as early as two o'clock in the afternoon to deposit their picnic hampers, thus securing a table.

Another new trend is the number of firms who now operate a complete picnicking service. One small local catering organization has a sole concession to supply picnics to members of the public direct to Glyndebourne. They deliver a large log basket covered with a pretty cloth, in which all the food, cutlery, crockery, glasses, etc., for the picnic are packed. At the end of the interval the repacked basket is simply returned to the cloakroom for collection. Many caterers in London as well as local hotels provide clients with complete hampers, tables, cloths, chairs and all the trimmings. Fortnum and Mason have a service entitled 'The Idyllic Picnic' for which you get a Vintage Rolls Royce and butler as well as the fitted hamper of goodies.

To some of the audience and particularly to some of the older Members of the Festival Society, many of whom have been loyal picnickers of the early school for years, the trend towards these more flamboyant and elaborate picnics may seem regrettable. However, most of the audience only come to Glyndebourne once a year and they will wish to make that evening as special as they can. After all, when urging his audience to wear evening dress at the first Festival John Christie insisted, 'We have spared nothing to provide opera of the highest standard – now you must make an effort too.' So whether it's on a rug eating delectable smoked salmon sandwiches or at a table with candles and caviar the Glyndebourne picnic – sandwiched as it is between hours of glorious music – should be an experience of the purest delight.

THE PICNICS

In recipes please note that, unless stated otherwise, flour is plain flour and spoon measures are level. For advice on such matters as equipment, packing, wrapping and so on, see 'Technical Department' on page 119.

AFTERNOON TEA

No doubt it is something to do with the fact that from the moment you descend the tree-shaded hill, turn through the gates and set eyes upon the tweed-hatted car park attendant, you can shut away the ugliness of the real world and indulge in being uniquely and magnificently English, and there can be no lovelier place for tea in summer than the garden at Glyndebourne. Bees buzz in the blue border, the scent of tobacco plants and an occasional old French rose mingle with the aroma of jasmine tea and the pepper of strawberries, and the lawns under the trees are dappled in sunlight. The very special type of opera-lover who takes a tranquil cup of tea at four o'clock knows from long experience that it is an ideal time to enjoy Glyndebourne's outdoor magic: the crowds have yet to arrive, and apart from birdsong and the gentle clink of silver against china, all is quiet. Even the trilling of rehearsing divas from the Green Room windows has ceased.

Yet the habit of afternoon tea might never have entered our lives had not an incredibly greedy aristocrat been caught gorging herself in the private confines of her boudoir in late eighteenth-century England. Legend has it that as the time between breakfast and dinner lengthened in the lighter months, Anna, Seventh Duchess of Bedford, unable to await the immense repast she enjoyed at her laden dinner table, demanded of her servants slivers of bread and butter, macaroons, almond cheesecakes and other niceties upon which she feasted.

Her secret was soon exposed, but, far from ridiculing her, as might well have happened in back-biting eighteenth-century society, other ladies emulated her habit. Concealing screens were cast aside; teapot and caddy, cup and saucer,

Asparagus Rolls with Hollandaise Sauce

Mini Bridge Rolls topped with Sardine, Chestnut and Capers

Sandwiches:
Smoked Chicken and Belgian Endive in White Bread
Curried Egg in Brown Bread
Stir-fried Salmon and Ginger in Brioche Bread with Walnut and Orange

Cheddar Cheese and Hazelnut Shortbreads

Madeleines
Marzipan Strawberries
Dark Coffee Cake

Raspberries and Cream

Champagne Tea Fizz

AFTERNOON TEA

motespoon and strainer, creamer and cakestand were unveiled for all to enjoy. Afternoon tea as a national tradition had begun, and any hostess wishing to be part of fashionable society partook, if she was to remain a lady of status and substance.

As twentieth-century fast food and a help-yourself style of service make irreversible inroads into our lives, ridding us of so many of our pleasant traditions, taking tea not the least of them, perhaps this is an occasion for a touch of nostalgia. Now, thanks to the Duchess, you can enjoy an Afternoon Tea Picnic with a full English flavour about it. Perhaps you will choose the sophistication of a simple menu: cool, crisp cucumber sandwiches, a feather-light scone and a sliver of Lemon Cake. Or, taken out of time, so to speak, you will decide upon my more elaborate menu. Whichever, the setting is perfect.

Asparagus rolls with Hollandaise Sauce

12 asparagus tips, lightly cooked

½ pt (275 ml) Hollandaise Sauce

Spread slices of crusted brown bread with Hollandaise Sauce. Place one fat or two or three slim asparagus tips on the front edge of each slice and roll up the slices tightly.

Cut the roll into two pieces with a diagonal stroke of the knife to give an interesting pointed shape.
Makes 20–24 pin-wheels

Sardine, chestnut and capers topping for mini bridge rolls

1 × 4 oz (110 g) tin sardines in tomato

6 chestnuts, cooked and shredded, or use drained chestnuts in brine, chopped

1 tbsp capers, drained

lemon juice

salt

milled pepper

Fillet and bone the sardines. Mash them with a fork. Mix in the chestnuts and capers. Season sparingly with lemon juice, salt and milled pepper.

The Sandwiches

Many cookery writers today are bidding us use fresh, crisp, crusty breads of a French nature or, if not French, then made with gutsy wholemeal flour. All of which is a fine idea for making lusty sandwiches for the children's lunch-pack, for an office snack, or for post-football-match sustenance. This kind of sturdy, wholesome bread is designed to contain – and with some good degree of safety – robust fillings, with crisp lettuce leaves cascading out of the sides and mayonnaise brimming appetizingly over the edges. It is not, however, the ideal bread for making the delicate, mouthwatering finger sandwiches served at tea-time, or at an 'At Home' or cocktail party, or at a reception where elegant presentation is called for.

For such morsels was the English sandwich loaf created: square, flat-topped and with a soft, close-textured crumb which however can be quite difficult to cut into the thin slivers needed to make those delicate sandwiches.

Bread for sandwich-making is best home-made and when it is one day old. It helps to put the loaf into the freezer for an hour or two before cutting: this firms up the crumb. It is also easier to cut if you use a knife with a long, sharp, serrated blade – or you may like to try experimenting with an electric carving knife: after a little practice this can produce excellent results.

It is always easier to work with butters and spreads which are prepared in advance, are at room temperature and are soft. Spread the cut face of the loaf *before* slicing and de-crusting; a flexible small-bladed palette-knife is good for easy spreading.

When making pin-wheels, fluted, shaped or rolled sandwiches, have a dampened tea-towel ready. Take the bread from the freezer, cut off the crust and spread the cut face with butter. Then carefully cut the thinnest possible slices from the full *length* of the loaf. Done this way, the bread will not break up. Lay the slices side by side on the damp towel to prevent the bread drying and curling up at the corners; this will also facilitate the rolling up of a pin-wheel. If the next slice is too frozen, you will have to wait only a couple of minutes for it to become manageable. Fill the first slice and roll it up carefully but tightly. Put each roll into a suitable plastic bag for freezing or storing. Cut them into delicate ⅛ in (3 mm) discs which will thaw out in a matter of minutes and be absolutely fresh.

For elegant presentation, sandwiches should be crusted before being cut into squares, fingers, triangles or, when the occasion is special enough, cut into shapes using fancy biscuit- or scone-cutters. (These come in a variety of shapes: round, oval, diamond or heart-shaped.) In order not to be too wasteful, the filling should be contained as near as is feasible within the area of the shape. The off-cuts of the buttered bread can then be toasted in the oven on a baking tray and made into savoury breadcrumbs for use in some other dish.

To keep sandwiches moist, cover them with a piece of greaseproof paper, wetted and lightly wrung out. Then cover the plate or tray with plastic film before refrigerating.

Sandwiches which are made a day in advance, but which you do not wish to freeze, should be packed in plastic bags to avoid contamination with other foodstuffs in your refrigerator.

Quantity guide for sandwiches

An average loaf – 2 lb (900 g) in weight, 4 × 4 in (10 × 10 cm) square – will yield 20–24 slices, depending on how deftly you cut the bread. This will make 10–12 sandwiches which, when quartered, will in turn give 40–48 squares or triangles.

* **To spread the bread slices fairly liberally and to the edges, you will require 8 oz (225 g) softened butter, creamed butter, or any of the other soft savoury and sweet spreads given in the book for 10–12 sandwiches.**
* **Soft spreadable fillings such as a fine pâté, meat, fish or cheese will require 8–10 oz (225–275 g) to fill 10–12 sandwiches.**
* **Fillings of a coarser nature, such as composite mixtures – crab mayonnaise, chopped chicken, flaked salmon, grated cheese with nuts or fruits, etc. – will require up to 12 oz (350 g) of filling for 10–12 sandwiches.**
* **Sliced meats: allow 1 oz (25 g) per sandwich, i.e. up to 12 oz (350 g) for 10–12 sandwiches.**
* **Allow 12 watercress leaves per sandwich.**
* **Allow 1 small lettuce leaf, de-veined, per sandwich.**
* **Mayonnaise or other 'flowing' spreads: allow a heaped teaspoon per sandwich, or 6 oz (175 g) for 10–12 sandwiches.**

Eventually it is up to the individual host or hostess to establish his or her own level of generosity. Sandwiches should be well and elegantly filled, but must be manageable for afternoon tea.
Note At tea-time, you may prefer to omit garlic or spring onions from sandwich fillings.

Smoked chicken and Belgian endive sandwiches

12 oz (350 g) smoked chicken fillet, skinned

2–3 tbsp double cream, to bind

salt and a little freshly ground pepper

1–2 heads of Belgian endive, split into leaves

In an old-fashioned mincer, mince the chicken and bind it to a spreadable paste with 2–3 tbsp double cream. Season to taste (be sparing with the salt). Spread white bread with tomato butter or plain butter. Spread a cushion of the smoked chicken paste on top, then add two or three crisp endive leaves.

Curried egg sandwiches

1 tsp curry paste or curry sauce

double cream to bind

6 hard-boiled eggs, sieved

salt and freshly ground pepper

Mix the curry paste or sauce with a little cream, then with the eggs. Season with salt and pepper. Spread brown or white bread with watercress butter, then top with the filling.

Stir-fried salmon and ginger sandwiches

1 × 12 oz (350 g) piece salmon, fresh or frozen

2 tbsp soya oil

1 in (2.5 cm) piece green ginger, peeled and finely chopped

1 small clove garlic, crushed

¼ tsp ground ginger

salt

lemon butter (see page 122)

Skin, bone and cut the salmon into ½ in (1 cm) cubes. In a large frying pan heat the oil until smoking well. Add the green ginger and garlic and fry for 10 seconds, stirring with a straight-edged wooden spatula to prevent burning. Add the salmon all at once. Spread it around and stir-fry it for 3–4 minutes, sprinkling with the ground ginger and salt. Remove the pan from the heat and let the fish cool completely. Reserve the pan juices.

In a liquidizer, make a purée of the fish, incorporating the pan juices. Give a little texture to the purée by using the stop/start method. Spread brioche bread with lemon butter. Spread a good cushion of the fish purée on it, and a few slivers of cucumber if liked.

Brioche bread with walnut and orange

This bread is also ideal for serving with starters at dinner time. It also makes a luxurious sandwich bread.

A

½ oz (15 g) yeast

2 tbs granulated sugar

4 fl oz (110 ml) warm water

4 eggs, well beaten

1½ tsp salt

20 oz (550 g) self-raising flour

5 oz (150 g) butter, melted

B

6 oz (175 g) walnuts or pecan halves, roughly but evenly crushed

zest of 1 orange

In a small basin combine the yeast and sugar with the warm water and allow to froth well.

Pour the eggs into a large bowl and mix in the yeast mixture. Add salt. Gradually incorporate the flour and the melted butter, using a wooden spoon and changing to using the hand if necessary as the mixture gets stiffer. Knead to a dough. Place this dough into a clean lightly-buttered bowl, rolling it around to coat the mass with a light film of butter. Cover with a clean cloth and put to prove in a warm place until doubled in volume – this takes about 1 hour.

Punch back the dough and knead very lightly. (Knead in the walnuts and zest if you are making this version.) Divide into two pieces and put into two lightly-buttered 450 g (1 lb) loaf tins. The dough will be soft and somewhat squidgy to handle.

Leave to rise again in a warm place for about an hour. Brush the tops with the following glaze:

1 egg yolk mixed with
2 tbs single cream

Bake in a pre-heated oven at 400°F(200°C) Reg 6 for 30–35 minutes when the loaves will be deep golden-brown and sound hollow when tapped. Cool. Wrap and freeze until ready for use.

To make the orange zest
Remove the zest using a swivel-blade potato-peeler. Gather into manageable piles and shred it as fine as you can with a knife. Blanch for a minute in boiling water. Cool under cold water, drain and pat dry with paper towels.

Cheddar cheese and hazelnut shortbreads

4 oz (110 g) plain white flour

½ tsp salt

tip of a pointed knife cayenne pepper

4 oz (110 g) unsalted butter

4 oz (110 g) mature Cheddar cheese, grated

2 oz (50 g) hazelnuts, lightly toasted, evenly but roughly crushed

Pre-heat the oven to 375°F (190°C) Reg 5. Sieve the flour with the salt and cayenne. Rub in the butter with the finger tips until sand-like in texture. Using a fork, mix in the grated cheese and crushed nuts. Knead to a soft pliable dough. Place 1 in (2.5 cm) knobs of the dough on a buttered baking sheet and press out with the floured tines of a fork.

Bake for 7–10 minutes or until crisp. Allow to set before moving to a wire rack. Pack carefully – in single layers – with a cushion of kitchen paper between layers.
Makes 25–30 bite-size shortbreads

Madeleines

4 eggs (90 g)

4 oz (110 g) caster sugar, sieved

1 tsp finely grated orange or lemon zest *or* 1 tsp rose *or* orange flower water

3½ oz (90 g) unsalted butter, melted but cool

3½ oz (90 g) self-raising flour, sieved twice

Pre-heat the oven to 375°F (190°C) Reg 5. In a bowl, using a rotary or hand whisk, whisk the eggs, sugar, zest or flower water until *thick* and pale and the whisk leaves a distinct trail when drawn across the mixture. Whisk in the cool melted butter, then lightly but thoroughly cut and fold in the flour.

Lightly butter and dredge with caster sugar two trays of bun tins or madeleine tins (these can be bought in specialist cook shops). Two-thirds fill them with the mixture. Bake for 10 minutes or until risen, golden brown and resistant to light pressure from your forefinger. Remove to a wire cooling tray. Depending on the size of your tins and on how hard you whisk (upon which will depend the volume of the mixture), you may need to make a third tray of the buns.
Makes 20–24 cakes

Marzipan strawberries

8 oz (225 g) caster sugar

4 fl oz (110 ml) water

tip of a tsp cream of tartar, dissolved in a little water

8 oz (225 g) ground almonds, sieved

small tsp rose water (triple strength) or lemon juice

red and green colouring

Bring the sugar and water to the boil. Add the cream of tartar. Continue boiling to a heat of 240°F (116°C), measured on an all-purpose food thermometer. Remove from the heat. Stir in the ground almonds and flower water and enough *drops* of colour to give a pretty strawberry pink. If you want to make different colours, then add the colouring at the kneading stage, having divided the paste into appropriate batches.

When cool, turn the paste on to a work surface dusted with icing sugar, and knead until smooth. Leave for a day or two to mature, wrapped in greaseproof paper and in an air-tight container in the refrigerator. Form into cylinders 1 in (2.5 cm) in diameter. Cut these into pieces and form into strawberry shapes. Leave to 'set'.

Make marzipan leaves using green colour in a little of the original marzipan, or clip plastic leaves off some suitable cheap plastic flowers. Artificial leaves can be purchased for this purpose. To arrive at a more realistic strawberry, meticulously mottle the surface of the formed 'fruits' using a small paint brush and red colouring.

Makes about 30–36 pieces

Dark coffee cake

10 oz (275 g) self-raising flour

1 tsp mixed spice

4 oz (110 g) unsalted butter, cubed

4 oz (110 g) Muscovado sugar

1 large egg, beaten

2 oz (50 g) golden syrup (approx, 2 tbsp), warmed in a teacup

2 fl oz (60 ml) strong coffee, cold

6 oz (175 g) sultanas or raisins

Pre-heat the oven to 325°F(160°C) Reg 3. Sieve the flour and spice into a bowl. Rub in the butter until you have a moist sand-like texture. Mix in the sugar. Make a well in the centre. Beat together the egg, syrup and coffee, and pour into the mixture. Gather the flour into the liquids using a fork. Beat well until you have a soft dropping consistency; add a little water if necessary. Stir in the dried fruit.

Line the base of a 7 in (18 cm) square, deep cake tin or an 8 in (20 cm) round one with buttered paper. Butter the sides of the tin. Spoon in the mixture, and level the top. Bake for 1¼–1½ hours or until the cake is firm to the touch and leaves the sides of the tin. Cool completely before turning out.

Champagne tea fizz

Take along a half-bottle of Cointreau

sugar syrup to taste

'sticks' of fresh pineapple for garnish

1 pt (575 ml) Yunnan or Keemun tea, made with ¾ oz (20 g) tea and *cold* water

1–2 bottles N.V. Champagne

curls of pared, oily orange zest

To make the cold clear infusion (which is fairly strong), pour a scant 'tot' of Cointreau into each champagne flute and a teaspoon or so of syrup. Add a stick of fresh pineapple. Half fill each glass with chilled tea. Top up with champagne, add a twist of zest so that the oils float on the surface.

Put the tea and cold water into a glass or china jug. Stir well and refrigerate overnight. Stir before going to bed and again when you get up. Strain and store in a *cold* thermos flask.

APPETISERS

Everyone should aim to arrive at Glyndebourne in time for a leisurely and calming stroll in the grounds before the performance begins. This can mean leaving London as early as two o'clock (or even earlier on Sundays) if heed is taken of the notice in the back of the programme to allow all of two hours' driving time *after* having crossed the Thames.

So, an early lunch has to be swallowed before putting on your glad rags for the journey south through the London suburbs and the delightful Sussex countryside beyond, with your picnic packed safely in the boot of the car. Some early birds may like to sip a cup of Earl Gray or even dip into a bowl of luscious strawberries in the tea tent; others prefer to pitch camp straight away and, having covered and anchored their boxes and baskets against the fickle weather, saunter around the top lake or examine the blue border for greenfly, pondering on the skill and artistry of the gardeners whose job it is to keep the beds so spick and span.

When you are lucky enough to strike a balmy evening it adds to the pleasure and romance of the occasion if you have taken along a bottle or two of champagne, chilled ready to be sipped from a tapering flute as you stroll and meander.

But what of the tit-bit, the appetiser, the canapé, hors d'oeuvre, call that tasty mouthful what you will, it does seem apt to produce some exciting bon-bouche or other from your Aladdin's box. My way of doing this has been to take with me something which guests can assemble themselves quickly and

Endive Spikes with Potted Tongue and Cashew Nuts

Marinated Potato Slices with Cottage Cheese and Keta

Black Figs with Soured Cream and Carpaccio

Smoked Fillet of Eel on Danish Rye Bread

Seveach of Monkfish with Water Chestnuts

Crab Claws with a spicy Tomato Cocktail Sauce

Mini-Tomatoes Stuffed with Curried Chicken and Chives

Hazelnut and Cheese Shortbreads

Gravadlax with Mustard Sauce on Fingers of Danish Rye Bread

easily: nothing too elaborate, you understand. Perhaps just the thinnest slivers of smoked salmon atop fingers of brown bread, or curls of carpaccio wrapped round quarters of ripe fig, a crisp finger of a melt-in-the-mouth savoury shortbread or a simple bowl of home-marinated Greek olives (though where does one put the stones?). By all means take the ubiquitous dip, but let the dip be an exotic one of soured cream, chives and shrimp – *sans ail* – or take a pot of the best Beluga caviar, transported to the *mise-en-scène* in a thermos of crushed ice.

But what if your imagination has failed you? Then read on for twenty unusual ideas for appetizers you can readily pop in your hamper to delight your guests on the lawns before the performance begins.

Endive spikes with potted tongue and cashew nuts

8 oz (225 g) lamb's tongue, cooked

2 oz (50 g) unsalted butter

1 tbsp Jamaican or Demerara Rum

1 heaped tsp mild French mustard

2 oz (50 g) salted cashew nuts, crushed

3 oz (75 g) clarified butter (optional)

1 extra ¼ in (6 mm) thick slice of tongue

leaves of Belgian endive

Cut the slice of tongue into small, ¼ in (6 mm) dice. Set aside. Put the tongue, butter, rum and mustard into a blender or food processor and make a fine paste. Scrape this into a bowl and mix in the diced tongue and crushed cashew nuts. Scrape into an attractive dish. Spoon over a thin film of clarified butter if used. Refrigerate until ready for use.

Pack leaves of washed and dried Belgian endive in a plastic bag. Spread some of the potted tongue on the base of each leaf and arrange fan-wise on a platter, or let your guests spread their own.

Makes 12 oz (350 g), so freeze some for future use if liked.

Marinated potato slices with cottage cheese and keta

For 4 guests

Allow one 2 in (5 cm) long potato per guest

2 oz (50 g) cottage cheese

1 oz (25 g) Keta (red salmon caviar)

Marinade for potatoes

2 tbsp olive oil

1 tbsp lemon juice

scant level tsp caster sugar

salt and milled pepper

Select four even-sized potatoes to yield four nice ¼ in (6 mm) thick slices from each. (Discard the ends.) Boil the potatoes in their skins, leaving them just crisp. Drain, peel and slice on the diagonal. Put these into a bowl, pour over the marinade and toss well. Leave to cool in this.

Pack the potatoes in a plastic box or attractive dish. Cover with plastic film. Refrigerate until ready for use or transporting.

Ease the lid off the caviar. Chill well. Transport in a cool box.

Transfer the cheese to an attractive container. Chill, transport in a cool box.

Either let your guests make up their own canapés or top potato slices with cream cheese and a little Keta.

Black figs with soured cream and carpaccio

Allow per serving

1 fig, quartered

4 thin slivers of carpaccio (or Parma Ham or Bressaolo)

1 small tub of soured cream is enough for 4–6 servings

milled pepper

Quarter the figs and pack them in one layer for transport. Arrange the slivers of ham on a small platter. Cover both with plastic film.

Let guests make up their own tit-bit by adding a blob of cream, a screw of the pepper mill and a sliver of ham to each quarter fig.

Smoked fillet of eel on Danish rye bread

allow 1 slice of rye bread per serving

chive or watercress butter (see pages 121 or 123)

allow 1½–2 × 6 in (15 cm) fillets of smoked eel per serving

quartered lemon or limes, wrapped in muslin

peppermill

Spread each slice of rye bread with the butter. Cut into three fingers or four squares. Lay over slivers of eel. Pack flat or on a platter covered with plastic film. Guests can add drops of lemon juice and/or pepper at will.

Seveach of monkfish with water chestnuts

6 oz (175 g) piece monkfish tail

12 water chestnuts, halved equatorwise

1 heaped tbsp chopped parsley

cocktail sticks

Marinade

strained juice of ½ orange

strained juice of 2 limes

2 tbsp olive oil

plenty of salt and milled pepper to taste

3–4 dashes Tabasco sauce, or a good pinch of cayenne pepper

Trim the monkfish tail of all skin and membrane. Cut it in half lengthways, cut each half into 1 in (2.5 cm) pieces. Mix well together all the ingredients for the marinade in a glass or china bowl. Add the fish and water chestnuts and parsley. Toss well. Cover with plastic film and leave overnight in the refrigerator.

To transport, spike pieces of fish and water chestnut onto cocktail sticks. Pack into a serving bowl with the marinade. Cover with plastic film. Transport in a cool box.

Crab claws with a spicy tomato cocktail sauce

Allow 2–3 defrosted crab claws per person, or use 2–3 jumbo prawns, shelled, split, de-veined.

Cocktail Sauce for 4–6 guests

¼ pt (150 ml) soured cream

1 tsp freshly grated (or bottled) horseradish

level tbsp tomato ketchup

2–3 cocktail gherkins, finely chopped

1 tbsp capers, drained, finely chopped

2–3 dashes Tabasco sauce

Mix all the ingredients together, spoon into an attractive container, cover with plastic film. Refrigerate until ready for transporting.

To serve, hold each crab claw by the point of the shell. Spoon a blob of the sauce onto the flesh and bite!

Mini-tomatoes stuffed with curried chicken and chives

3–4 tomatoes per serving

Filling

1 plump, skinned and boned chicken breast

1 tbsp olive oil for frying

1 good tsp mild curry powder

salt and pepper

1 tbsp mango or other chutney, chopped

whisky – one 'double' measure

3 tbsp double cream

2 tbsp mayonnaise

1 tbsp snipped chives

Slice the chicken into strips, then cut across into tiny cubes. Heat the oil until lightly smoking. Stir-fry the chicken strips, sprinkling with curry powder, salt and pepper as you do so, for 2–3 minutes. Add the chutney. Stir in. Pour over the whisky, then the cream. Bubble for 1–2 minutes until viscous. Cool. Make a rough purée of the mixture in a blender, using the stop-start technique. Stir in the mayonnaise and chives. Fill into emptied tomato shells.

To prepare the tomatoes, invert each tomato. Cut off a ¼ in (6 mm) top and reserve. Using the handle end of a teaspoon scoop out and discard the seeds. Season the inside lightly with salt and pepper.

Fill with the curried chicken mixture. Pop on a top. Pack, and refrigerate until ready to transport.

Hazelnut and cheese shortbreads

4 oz (110 g) butter

3 oz (75 g) flour

2 oz (50 g) hazelnuts, rubbed and crushed

4 oz (110 g) Cheddar cheese, grated

1 egg yolk

1 egg white, whisked

crystals of sea salt

Optional garnish

extra hazelnuts

Rub the butter into the flour until sand-like in texture. Toss in the crushed hazelnuts and grated cheese. Mix in the egg yolk and gather the mixture together. Knead lightly into a ball. Form into a square. Place the dough onto a non-stick or buttered baking sheet. Press or roll to a square ½ in (5 cm) thick. Mark with a knife into 2 × 1 in (2.5 cm) fingers. Brush the surface of the dough with beaten egg white. Scatter over a little sea salt or press a whole hazelnut into each finger. Bake at 400°F (200°C) Reg 6 for 10–12 minutes or until crisp and brown. Leave to cool somewhat before lifting to a wire cooling rack.
Makes 20–24 fingers

Gravadlax with mustard sauce on fingers of Danish rye bread

Purchase the Gravadlax or substitute slivers of smoked halibut or smoked turbot. Lightly butter pieces of rye bread and cut into three fingers, crossways. Lay curls of Gravadlax on top, dribble over a little of the sauce or let guests do this for themselves. Tuck a frond of freshly picked dill in and amongst.

Mustard sauce for gravadlax

3 tsp mild French mustard

¼ tsp dry English mustard

2 tsp caster sugar

1 dsp red or white wine vinegar

2 tbsp soy oil

1 tbsp chopped dill fronds (optional)

Using a small balloon whisk, mix all the ingredients to a smooth sauce.

THE VERY ENGLISH PICNIC

There is something almost unnervingly English about the scene at Glyndebourne as, during the dinner interval, you meander towards the ha-ha to find the brown and white cows rhythmically chewing the cud (surely in 4/4 time?) and studying your approach. Behind their bovine stare, they appear to be naïvely waiting to see what is revealed from under your draped table, or out of your hamper.

It would be tantamount to sacrilege were you to unveil bowls of Tabbouleh or a dish of spicy cold Koftas. Even a platter of Gravadlax would mar the unique Englishness of this tranquil setting. The faint bleating of the sheep – now withdrawn to the middle distance – and an early evening sun low in the sky, whose light suffuses the lawns with pale gold: this is England at its most magical. Thought to be too idyllic to exist by most English people, yet eagerly anticipated by visitors from abroad already acquainted with Constable's paintings, it is a setting which is painted by every artist who wants to preserve for posterity this sylvan Sussex splendour.

At a more appropriate time of day, this is also the perfect setting for Afternoon Tea, but now the timing and the surroundings are exactly right for that most English of picnics: cool, pink succulent salmon served with a crisp green salad of those familiar shell-shaped leaves, neatly dressed with lemon and honey. A time for serving those yellow waxy-textured Jersey potatoes, cooked until just tender but still whole, or an occasion to enjoy the exotic Pink Fir Apple potato lightly coated with cream and sprinkled with apple mint, equally delicious hot or cold.

English strawberries were designed for such a supper. Deep crimson, pointed and peppery-nosed, arranged in one vast heap, their strong green hulls waiting to be gently secured in the fingers before being dipped, first in powdered sugar,

Old English Potted Salmon with Brown Bread and Butter or Crackers

---

Terrine of Wild Duck with Muscatel Raisins and Rum

Pink Fir Apple Potato Salad

Tomato, Carrot and Orange Salad

New Summer Pudding with a Raspberry 'Cullis'

or

Gooseberry Fool with Roseflower Water

then in thick buttery cream. During those brief few weeks when the red berry fruits are in season together, our own special Summer Pudding – simple to make and unique to visitors from afar – might well have pride of place. A finger, but no more, of a fine cheese: perhaps an earthy-toned Cheshire, a sliver of sharp Stilton or a taste of leafy-scented Blue Vinney from Dorset might well find a place at the end of such fare.

It would not be unimaginable to bring along a decanter of white port – best chilled, mind you – or a pretty Sauternes, also packed round with ice, its buttery flavour making an exact marriage with the light acid-earthiness of the cheese, leaving you in a heady state and in just the right frame of mind to face the last act, of 'Falstaff' is it, or perhaps 'Albert Herring'?

If all of this is too familiar to you and you feel in a more adventurous mood yet want to stay with a very English theme, my menu here will slot into your plans admirably.

Old English potted salmon

You might like to try the original way of potting our king of fish.

1 lb (450 g) piece salmon
1 level tsp mace
pinch of ground clove
¼ tsp ground bay leaf, *or* 1 bay leaf broken into bits
1 slice lemon
salt
white pepper, freshly milled
7 oz (200 g) butter

Skin and slice the fish into thinnish pieces. Put into an earthenware pot just large enough to contain it, seasoning well with the herbs and spices, lemon and salt and pepper as you arrange the pieces, and dispersing 4 oz (110 g) butter amongst the fish pieces. Put a lid on the pot and stand this in a container of hot water. Bake at 400°F (200°C) Reg 6 until the fish is cooked (about 45 minutes). Cool completely. Make a purée in a food processor or blender. Pack this purée, having adjusted the seasoning if necessary, into an attractive china container. Chill well.

To clarify butter, put 3 oz (75 g) butter into a pan and add about ½ pt (275 ml) water. Bring to the boil, leave to cool, then put to set in the refrigerator. Remove the 'set' butter and wipe the underside clean with paper towel. Melt this butter again without it getting too hot. Pour over the chilled salmon purée and return the dish to the refrigerator to set again. Serve like a pâté.

Serves 6–8

Terrine of wild duck with muscatel raisins and rum

The powerful game flavour of this terrine is enhanced by the warmth of ginger and rum-scented raisins.

1 wild duck
1 slice (8 oz/225 g) raw gammon, ⅓ in (9 mm) thick
12 oz (350 g) fat belly pork, skinned
1 duck liver *or* 2 chicken livers
1 large *or* 2 small cloves of garlic, crushed
3 tsp gelatine crystals
1 large egg, beaten
3 oz (75 g) Californian raisins, soaked in 1 tbsp rum
⅛ pt (75 ml) light rum

¼ pt (150 ml) red burgundy-type wine

2 tsp ground ginger

1 tsp salt

1 tsp cracked *or* milled pepper

12 oz (350 g) streaky bacon, de-rinded, to line mould (optional)

Garnish (optional)

watercress

Skin and bone the duck. Use the carcass for game stock or gravy at some other time. Slice the breast across into ¼ in (6 mm) pieces. Dice half the gammon into ⅓ in (9 mm) pieces.

In a food processor, mince together the belly pork, duck-leg meat, livers, half slice of gammon and garlic, and sprinkle over the gelatine crystals, using the egg as liquid. Scrape into a bowl. Add the diced ham, sliced duck-breast and raisins. Pour over the rum and wine. Sprinkle over the ginger and seasoning and mix together well. Cover with plastic film and leave in the refrigerator overnight.

Turn the mixture into a terrine (bacon-lined if liked) and bake in a pre-heated oven at 400°F (200°C) Reg 6 in a deep bain marie for 1 hour. Leave to cool. Press with a foil-covered weighted board which just fits inside the edge of the terrine. Leave to set. Then unmould, using a heated palette knife. Garnish with watercress if liked.

Serves 8–10

Pink fir apple potato salad

An excellent accompaniment to cold roast meat. The hot potatoes absorb the flavour of the wine and oil.

1½ lb (700 g) Pink Fir Apple potatoes or waxy new potatoes, boiled and slightly cooled

1 × 5 fl oz (150 ml) glass dry white wine mixed with 2 tbsp olive oil

salt and milled pepper

2 small red-skinned onions, cut into rings

2 hard-boiled eggs, roughly chopped

Dressing

½ pt (275 ml) soured cream

1 heaped tsp mild French or English mustard (try Tewkesbury)

juice of ½ lemon

pinch of salt

Skin the potatoes if you like, and cut them into ¼ in (6 mm) discs. Splash them with the wine and oil while they are still warm. Season lightly and leave to cool and absorb the liquid. Mix with the onion rings (reserving some for a garnish) and the chopped hard-boiled eggs.

Make up the dressing and fold the potatoes into this in a large bowl. Chill for an hour, covered with plastic film.

Serves 6

Tomato, carrot and orange salad

2 beefsteak tomatoes

2 large navel oranges

2 large carrots, peeled

lettuce leaves

Dressing

¼ pt (150 ml) olive oil

⅛ pt (75 ml) nut oil

juice and grated rind of 1 orange

1 tbsp red wine vinegar

1 tsp mild French mustard

1 tsp caster sugar

salt

milled pepper

Skin, seed and cut the tomatoes into petals. Knife-peel the oranges and cut into segments. Grate the carrots on the julienne blade of a food processor or on the coarse side of a grater.

Make up the dressing by combining all the ingredients. Arrange the fruit and vegetables on lettuce leaves in individual bowls. Dress before serving or pass the dressing separately.

Serves 6

New summer pudding

The temptation to use cake in place of the traditional bread is difficult to resist, but I settle instead for a two-day-old, top-quality white Jewish bread. Made in an oblong mould or loaf tin, I serve this new version of an old favourite cut into ¾ in (2 cm) slices and topped with rich pouring cream and/or raspberry cullis. It is still best made when the three berries – raspberries, redcurrants and blackcurrants – are all available together.

Syrup

⅓ pt (200 ml) water

8 oz (225 g) sugar

juice of 1 lemon

2 sachets gelatine crystals

Pudding

8 oz (225 g) blackcurrants, or you can use strawberries, quartered

8 oz (225 g) raspberries

8 oz (225 g) redcurrants, picked over

enough thin slices of decrusted white bread to line the sides, base and top of your selected mould

Bring the first four ingredients for the syrup to boiling point, then gradually sprinkle over the gelatine crystals, whisking them until dissolved. Crush the blackcurrants with the butt of a rolling pin and combine with the raspberries and redcurrants in a large bowl. Pour over the hot syrup and leave to cool.

Line the base and sides of your chosen mould with the thin slices of bread and then, just as it is beginning to gel, ladle the fruit mixture in. Arrange a layer of bread slices on top. Put a weighted board on top to press the juices through the bread, and refrigerate overnight. Turn out on to a shallow dish to serve.

Serves 6–8

Raspberry cullis

12 oz (350 g) punnet of raspberries (or frozen)

4 oz (110 g) caster sugar

juice of ½ small lemon

1 tbsp gin or Kirsch

Purée all the ingredients in a blender, then rub through a fine sieve to remove the seeds. Chill well, covered with plastic film.

Serves 6–8

Gooseberry fool with roseflower water

1 lb (450 g) young green gooseberries

2 oz (50 g) unsalted butter

4 oz (110 g) or less sugar

1 tbsp triple-strength roseflower water

½ pt (275 ml) double cream

Top, tail and wash the gooseberries. Melt the butter without letting it take on any colour. Add the gooseberries, put on a lid and cook over a low heat for 10 minutes, or until soft. Remove from the heat and sweeten to taste. Add the roseflower water and mix in. Leave to cool.

Put the fruit through the fine grid of a mouli (a blender makes the purée too foamy). Whip the cream and fold into the cooled purée. Spoon into individual glasses. Chill, covered with Clingfilm.

Serves 6

THE TRAVELLER'S PICNIC

A sizeable proportion of the Glyndebourne audience come to the opera by train as it avoids the hassle of traffic jams and is generally much more relaxing. Indeed, the proportion is so large that the curtain never rises until the train contingent are safely in their seats – although this may be due to the fact that a number of the orchestra also travel by train. Imagine the management announcing from the stage that the first two bars of the overture to 'The Magic Flute' will be omitted because British Rail have engineering works at Balcombe and the trombones haven't turned up. But an individual driver's story of holdups and flat tyres will fall on deaf ears and he will be relegated to the Organ Room if he arrives late, to watch that unhappy substitute to the live stage – the closed-circuit television.

For some members of the audience even these advantages cannot compensate for the practical difficulties of bringing a good picnic by train. This is certainly true if you insist on the complex paraphernalia of a formal picnic – tables and chairs, umbrellas and large unwieldy picnic boxes; but a very luxurious meal (with no sandwiches involved) can be brought by two people on a train, and one of the party may even have the strength to carry a rug. If you do prefer to sit on chairs for your picnic you can either go straight to the marquee when you arrive at Glyndebourne to see if there is any room or, if the weather is good, make for one of the many benches in the gardens; there are always a number of chairs in the walled garden by Mildmay for those who have not brought their own. Take them to the lower of the two lawns where in June the Old Roses will be out. On one side you will get the wonderful scent of Roseraie de L'Haie and on the other an exquisite old pale pink rose with gently crumpled blooms and the absurdly romantic name *La cuisse de nymphe émue*.

This picnic may also suit those who are working during

Individual Cheese Mousses

Marinated Beef Salad with Green Peppercorns

Nectarines with Fresh Raspberry Sauce
Lemon Biscuits

the day, although the 'No-Cooking Picnic' (see page 62) may suit them better. Most of the dishes can be made the evening before and put in the fridge overnight and then, if possible, in the office fridge the next day (important in hot weather).

The formal picnicker looks haughtily down on such practical items as plastic boxes or Tupperware (now made in very stylish colours) but for this type of picnic they are strongly recommended. China or earthenware dishes are very heavy to carry far and by the time you have walked the length of the platforms on Victoria and Lewes stations you will heartily wish you had had the sense to forgo elegance for comfort. By all means take proper china plates and glasses if you prefer, although some plastic ones are now beautifully designed and very pretty, but the food can most definitely be in plastic. You should require no more than two baskets or bags for these picnics: one for the food (preferably an insulated box or bag) and one for the plates, glasses, knives, forks, napkins and the drink. Remember you have four hands between you and it is always easier to carry several light bags than to try to fit everything into one.

Individual cheese mousses

Many recipes for cheese mousses involve cream cheese with cream and consommé. This recipe which uses different cheeses is more robust and slightly richer. The type of cheese you use is a question of taste and if you like the recipe you can experiment. Use blue cheese and you have a different distinctive overall flavour than if you use Cheshire or Lancashire. You could also try it with a goat's cheese.

1 tsp powdered gelatine

6 oz (175 g) hard cheese (Cheshire, Lancashire, Stilton)

2 fl oz (60 ml) dry white wine

1 small clove garlic

½ tsp Dijon mustard

¼ tsp curry powder

12 oz (350 g) curd cheese

salt, pepper, Tabasco sauce

5 oz (150 g) carton double cream

chopped chives for garnish

Dissolve the gelatine into half a teacup of hot water and leave to cool. Take the rind off the cheese if necessary and crumble it into a blender. Add the wine, crushed garlic, mustard and curry powder and process until smooth. Add the cooled gelatine and the curd cheese and mix again until completely smooth. Add salt, pepper and Tabasco to taste, and pour into a large bowl. Whip the cream until fairly thick and fold into the cheese mixture. Pour into the ramikins and put into the fridge until set. Sprinkle chopped chives on top before covering each one in cling film and putting it in the picnic box.

Marinated beef salad with green peppercorns

The beauty of this salad, apart from tasting delicious, is that it is complete in itself as a main course. All you need in addition is a bag of crisp lettuce sprinkled with fresh herbs and a roll or bread if you wish. The celeriac is optional as it is not always easy to buy.

12 oz (350 g) lean good-quality frying steak, about 2 in (5 cm) thick

Marinade

2 tbsp olive oil

3 tbsp red wine vinegar

1 tbsp soy sauce

½ small onion, chopped

rind of 1 orange, grated

1 tsp fresh thyme, dried or chopped

Salad

6 oz (175 g) new potatoes, peeled

1½ oz (40 g) carrots julienned into matchsticks

2 spring onions, thinly sliced including some of the green

2 tbsp Italian parsley, chopped

1½ oz (40 g) celeriac, julienned into matchsticks

1½ oz (40 g) green pepper, julienned into matchsticks

1½ oz (40 g) red pepper, julienned into matchsticks

Dressing

1 dsp Dijon mustard

1 egg yolk

1 clove garlic, crushed

1 tbsp red wine vinegar

salt and pepper

1 tsp whole green peppercorns

5 tbsp good olive oil

Green salad

1 bag young lettuce leaves

watercress

chopped herbs

Put the beef into a dish into which it just fits. Mix together all the ingredients for the marinade and pour over the beef. Leave for three to four hours turning it occasionally. Using a melon scoop or very small teaspoon make the potatoes into little balls (you can dice them but they will not look so nice in the salad). Bring them to the boil in salted water and cook until tender – about 5 minutes. Watch carefully as they mustn't go mushy. Drain and leave to cool.

Boil the carrots, spring onions/parsley, the celeriac and peppers in a separate pan for 1 minute. Drain immediately and refresh under cold running water. Leave to cool.

Remove the beef from the marinade. Heat a very heavy skillet or frying pan, paint with oil and fry the beef over the highest possible heat for about 5 minutes on each side or until medium-rare. It should be almost charred on the outside and lusciously juicy inside. Leave to cool slightly and cut it into plump matchsticks (about ¼–½ in (6–12 mm) thick.

Make the dressing by putting the mustard into a small bowl. Add the egg yolk and mix very well. Add the crushed garlic, vinegar, salt, green peppercorns and oil, mixing well until it is all amalgamated. Pour the dressing into a large bowl. Add the beef, potatoes, onions, peppers, carrots and parsley and mix thoroughly and carefully. Put covered into the fridge until ready to pack for the picnic. Transfer into a plastic bowl with a lid and put in the picnic basket.

Take along with a bag of crisp young lettuce leaves, carefully picked-over watercress and fresh mixed chopped herbs. When ready to serve the picnic let your guests put some of the lettuce on their plates, then spoon the beef salad on top. Serve with crusty bread or rolls.

Nectarines with fresh raspberry sauce

2 fresh juicy nectarines (they must be fully ripe)

juice of 1 lemon

8 oz (225 g) fresh raspberries

caster sugar

gin

Peel and slice the nectarines into a bowl. Pour the lemon over and mix. Put the raspberries through a sieve or mouli, add sugar to taste and a splash of gin. Pour the raspberry sauce over the nectarines, cover and chill.

To transport, put them in a plastic bowl or box with a lid and pack them in the picnic box close to the ice sachet. Take a small pot of cream to eat with them, and some biscuits if you have room. The Lemon Biscuits (below), though rather breakable, are exquisite.

Serves 2

Lemon biscuits

6 oz (175 g) butter

2 oz (50 g) caster sugar

8 oz (225 g) self-raising flour

rind of 2 lemons, finely grated

Cream the butter and sugar, add the flour into which you have grated the lemon rind and mix together with your hands until you have a ball of dough. Roll out on to a floured board to ¼ in (6 mm) thick, using more flour if it seems to get too sticky, and cut into rounds, hearts or whatever shape takes your fancy. Place them on lightly greased baking sheets and bake in a moderate oven for 8–10 minutes or until pale and golden. Cool on a tray and sprinkle with a little icing sugar.

THE TAIL-GATE PARTY

Tail-gating is a way of picnicking peculiar to American ball games, when shooting brakes, hatchbacks, station wagons, call them what you will, are dovetailed into parking lots outside college stadiums. Food and drink are dispensed from the boot – sorry, trunk – whilst the participants stand, slouch, or sit around.

From Princeton to Yale, the game has become secondary to this 'potlatch' ceremony, which starts hours before kick-off as old graduates from far and wide gradually re-unite, manifesting their recently acquired wealth.

From what I have seen of tail-gating with Yale alumni friends, it is more of an *alfresco* sit-down affair at the rear of the car (mercifully without the engine running, unlike here in Britain, where I have actually seen people picnicking on the central reservations of the M4, engulfed in fumes). I did wonder, back in 1981, why we had left the turnpike at New Haven for the famous Yale Bowl (stadium) a full two hours before the (dreaded) game was due to commence. Of course I hadn't known what was in store, and how long it would take to create this socially vital *mise-en-scène*. Hammacher-Schlemmer and Bloomingdales stores must have been stripped bare and I swear some of these guys had been to England, if not Glyndebourne itself, to judge from the way the tables were set up and draped, 'designer' canvas chairs unfolded, portable barbecues lit, and flowers, candelabra, place mats, napkins and wine coolers distributed around. All this in full midwinter and in a car park in New Haven, which is no beauty spot I promise you.

Essential to the success of a tail-gate party, other than an abundant supply of liquor in the form of Scotch or Bourbon and cases of beers, is something, almost anything, hot. It might be a soup, a stew, grilled steaks, burgers or hot dogs (the smell of charring meat on the frosty air was particularly memorable).

The American sandwich also has its place in a tail-gate menu. The authentic version has mounds (and I mean mounds,

The Cold Smithburger

Raised Pork and Cranberry Pie
Spinach and Mushroom Salad with Bacon

Brownies

as those who know the States will bear out) of rare roast beef, pastrami, ham, cheese and chicken, liberally garnished with tomatoes, radishes, cucumbers and sweet pickles and blopped with mayonnaise. Brownies and Apple Pie belong by right; and ice cream is no hassle to take along. All good stuff on a cold day.

You, too, can enjoy a tail-gate style picnic right here at Glyndebourne if you have a mind to, up in the car park (50p at current rates). I know you can, I've seen it done!

The Cold Smithburger

Louis' in New Haven, Connecticut, claims to be the originator of the hamburger in America back in the 1880s. Still in full swing today, this tiny family-run business uses the original nineteenth-century vertical gas grills for cooking and, more interestingly, the finished burger is served in toasted bread, not the soft pappy sesame roll we have come to expect. I, too, prefer mine in toast.

1 lb (450 g) green gammon, coarsely minced

1 lb (450 g) white raw chicken meat, coarsely minced

salt and white pepper

pinch of mace

16 toasts, cut into rounds with a large pastry-cutter, buttered or dry

Mix the meats, season and shape. Grill or pan-fry the burgers. Serve sliced, cold, with relishes of your choice: tomato sauce, apple chutney, sweetcorn or onions.
Makes 8 × 3 in (7.5 cm) burgers

Raised pork and cranberry pie

Pie crust

4 oz (110 g) lard

2 oz (50 g) butter

1 lb (450 g) flour

1 oz (25 g) icing sugar

1 tsp salt

¼ tsp ground mace

1 tsp orange zest, finely grated

Filling

2½ lb (1.1 kg) lean pork meat, coarsely minced

12 oz (350 g) pork fat, coarsely minced

1 tsp orange zest, grated

1 tsp ground mace

1 good tsp salt

1 tsp milled pepper

6 oz (175 g) Ocean Spray cranberries

Jelly

aspic crystals

gelatine crystals

¼ pt (150 ml) Amontillado sherry

To make the pie crust, bring the lard, butter and ⅓ pt (200 ml) water to the boil in a pan. In a large bowl, sieve the flour, sugar, salt, pepper and mace together (but not the orange zest; add this after sieving). Make a well. Pour in the liquid butter and lard mixture at one fell swoop. Mix it to a soft dough with a fork and leave to cool a little. Butter an 8 in (20 cm) round 2 in (5 cm) deep loose-bottomed tin.

Knead the dough lightly on a floured work surface. Cut one-third off and retain for the lid of the pie. Roll out the larger piece to a circle 14–15 in (35–38 cm) in diameter. Fold into four and place in the tin. Unfold and press into place, up and over the edge of the tin.

Mix the meat, fat, zest, mace, salt and pepper together well. Then mix in the cranberries. Spoon the filling into the pastry case. Fold over the edge. Wet the edges. Roll and fit the lid, pinching the edges together. Apply any decorations, such as leaves, circles and flutes. Make a small hole in the centre and fit a foil funnel to allow steam to escape.

Stand the tin on a tray and bake in a pre-heated oven at 400°F (200°C) Reg 6 for 1 hour. Lower the temperature to 350°F (180°C) Reg 4 and bake for a further 1 hour. Remove the ring but not the base. Brush the pie all over with beaten egg. Return it to the oven for a further 30 minutes. Leave it to cool before removing the base.

When the pie is quite cold, make up 1 pt (575 ml) of commercial aspic jelly, following the instructions on the packet but substituting half the aspic crystals for plain gelatine crystals and using ¾ pt (425 ml) boiling water and ¼ pt (150 ml) Amontillado sherry for extra flavour. Leave this to cool to the point when it is just beginning to gel, then pour into the pie through the hole in the lid, using a small funnel. The amount of jelly to pour through the funnel depends on how much your pastry lid has or has not risen and how much your meat has shrunk. Serve hot or cold. *Serves 8–10*

Spinach and mushroom salad with bacon

12 rashers streaky bacon

4 slices white bread, ½ in (1.2 cm) thick

butter for frying

1 lb (450 g) spinach, washed and de-veined

8 oz (225 g) very white tight-capped mushrooms

Dressing

¼ pt (150 ml) nut oil

1 tsp mild French mustard

juice of ½ lemon

salt and pepper

1 tsp caster sugar

⅛ pt (75 ml) single cream

Garnish

sprigs of parsley

De-rind the bacon and cut into small pieces. Dry-fry until really crisp. Remove the crusts from the bread and cut into ½ in (1.2 cm) cubes. Either fry in the bacon fat, adding a little butter if necessary, or fry in butter alone for good flavour. Cool. The secret of a good nutty-flavoured, well-coloured crouton is very slow frying, adding enough butter or oil for them to absorb, and moving them about all the time they are frying – tedious, but well worth the effort. (Croutons freeze well and can be kept in store for soups and other uses.)

Make up the dressing in the usual way, adding the cream last. Break up the spinach leaves into bite-sized pieces, and arrange a bed of these in individual bowls. Divide the bacon and croutons evenly between the bowls. Wipe and thinly slice the raw mushrooms and pile these on top of each salad.

Garnish with sprigs of parsley. Add the dressing at the table so that everything stays crisp.
Serves 4

Brownies

There are many different recipes for Brownies, some more 'cakey' than others. I prefer mine to be chewy, and this is what these are. They are also quite sweet – and all the better for that, too

4 oz (110 g) dark chocolate

4 oz (110 g) butter

12 oz (350 g) caster sugar

1 tsp vanilla essence

2 eggs, lightly beaten

4 oz (110 g) self-raising flour sieved with ½ tsp salt

4–6 oz (110–175 g) walnuts, roughly crushed

Butter and line an 8 in (20 cm) square tin. Soften the chocolate in a bowl over hot water. Beat in the butter away from the heat. Beat in the sugar and essence. Beat in the eggs a little at a time. Quickly stir in the flour and salt. Fold in the nuts.

Spoon and spread evenly into the cake tin. Bake at 350°F (180°C) Reg 4 for 35–40 minutes. Allow to cool slightly and cut into squares. Store in an airtight tin. Brownies can be frozen.
Makes about 16 squares

THE STAND-UP PICNIC

Squatting or sitting on grass to eat, no matter what the occasion, is for children. For the average adult, if he or she is honest, it is crippling to the muscles – well, to mine it is – and you end up with grass stains on your trouser knees or skirt front as perforce you kneel to serve your assembled dishes. You also acquire a wet posterior as you miss your allotted square foot of rug when flopping out of control to the ground. And is that a cowpat underneath? Henry is so careless when he lays a rug! The merest tilt in the landfall of your chosen site creates further discomfort: the list to port or starboard requiring the added use of an elbow if you are not to topple over completely.

Almost any position on the ground is potentially undignified and certainly impractical when it comes to eating. Even if you have become adept at striking a Roman pose, just how do you use a fork and hold a glass, when one hand is elegantly but irretrievably taken up as a flying buttress to this arrangement? And how – once past the age of 35 – do you get up again without the aid of others, who may well be in the same plight? There is only one way. You roll over, stagger to your knees and heave yourself up. Really, *it is just not on*!

This is why the stand-up picnic is here. Happily it does not automatically entail a menu limited to sandwiches or finger food. It does mean, however, that all food must be 'forkable'. It has to be cut up and presented in such a way that no wayward morsel misses the mouth at first strike; there must be no recalcitrant lettuce leaves or alfalfa sprouts, no

Angel Biscuits
Brioche Sandwiches with Gravadlax

Filo Pastries with Mussels, Tomato and Herbs

Fingers of White Bread, spread with Watercress Butter and Smoked Halibut

---

Cherry Tomatoes with Soured Cream and Keta

Simple Stuffed Half Eggs with Tarragon

Cold Spiced Chicken Striplets

Black Figs with Mascapone Cheese and Prosciutto

Individual Beef Tartares on Rye Discs

Marrons Glacés
Turkish Delight
Marinated Fingers of Crystallized Pineapple and Melon

THE STAND-UP PICNIC

dripping dressings, no skin or wayward gristle, no inedible garnishes and certainly no bones – so any mousse you might prepare has to be sieved I'm afraid.

It so happens that fork food, when carefully confected is *the* most delicious food to take on a picnic, with the additional benefit that it can be attractively arranged at home and will arrive in good visual state. A pretty 8 in (20 cm) plate is about the right size and weight to carry in the hand (you don't *have* to have a glass with you – that can rest on a nearby wall).

Fork food, elegantly arranged on a table, releases you to meander as far from the assembled collation as you wish: down to the lake; through to explore the mysteries of the gardens; to watch a soothing match on the croquet lawn or to hover near the Green Room window for a preview of the Count's contribution to the last act of whichever opera is to follow your repast.

Angel biscuits

These versatile little cocktail scones are best eaten soon after baking: split and spread with butter and slivers of oak-smoked ham or turkey, prosciutto or Gravadlax. They can also be eaten at tea-time, straight from the oven, spread with clotted cream and home-made raspberry preserve or damson cheese.

The butter brushed onto the top keeps the crust soft. If you choose to serve them with some unusual smoked fish such as turbot or halibut, then include a teaspoon of finely grated lemon zest in the mixture (mix this well into the yoghurt).

1 tsp dried yeast creamed in 1 tbsp blood-warm water

8 oz (225 g) self-raising flour

½ oz (15 g) caster sugar

1 tsp salt

2 oz (50 g) unsalted butter, fridge-hard and diced

¼ pt (150 ml) strained Greek yoghurt

⅛ pt (75 ml) milk

1 oz (25 g) cool, melted butter

Pre-heat the oven to 425°F (220°C) Reg 7. Cream the yeast in a cup. On a food processor blend the flour, sugar, salt and butter until sand-like in texture. Turn onto a board. Make a well.

Mix the proved yeast with the yoghurt. Tip into the well with the milk and gather in the flour. Knead to a soft dough. Roll out to ¾ in (2 cm) thick. Cut into small, 1½ in (4 cm) circles. Brush the tops with melted butter. Arrange on a buttered baking sheet. Bake at 425°F (220°C) Reg 7 for 12–15 minutes, then pack into bags and freeze, or open-freeze. Eat the same day.

Makes 24

Brioche sandwiches with gravadlax

Sweet-creamed butter
6 oz (175 g) softened butter
1 oz (25 g) soft brown sugar
1 tsp mild French mustard
2 tsp lemon juice
Bread
1 × 1 lb (450 g) oblong, not fluted, loaf brioche (see page 22)
Filling
8 oz (225 g) Gravadlax, thinly sliced
1 tbsp finely snipped chives or parsley
⅛ pt (75 ml) special sauce (which you buy with the Gravadlax)

Beat together all the ingredients for the butter. Cut and spread with the special butter 12 slices of the brioche bread. This is easier to do if you butter the crumb surface before cutting, and if the bread is semi-frozen.

Lay a good cushion of Gravadlax slices on six of the slices. Sprinkle with chives or parsley. Fit the top piece of bread. Trim off the crusts. Cut into manageable fingers or squares, using a serrated (not saw-toothed) knife. Dribble over a little of the special sauce.

Makes 6 rounds (12 fingers or 24 small squares)

Filo pastries with mussels, tomato and herbs

1 box Filo pastry
melted butter
24 mussels, well washed
3 tomatoes, skinned, seeded, cut into 8 pieces each
1 heaped tbsp parsley, finely chopped
2 oz (50 g) butter
juice of ½ lemon, strained
small clove garlic, crushed
salt
milled pepper

In a large lidded pan, bring to a rapid boil 1-in of salted water. Tip in the washed mussels, fit the lid and toss well, steaming the mussels open (about 2–3 minutes). Drain in a colander. Cool. Shell, discarding the black beard from each mussel.

Melt the butter in a pan until *warm*. Add the tomato and simmer until soft. Drain, retaining juices. Return the juices to the pan, add garlic and lemon juice and bubble until syrupy. Cool. Mix in the tomato, parsley and mussels.

Pre-heat the oven to 400°F (200°C) Reg 6. Having ready a dampened kitchen cloth, wrung out, place three layers of Filo pastry on a work surface. Brush liberally with melted butter. Cut into 8 squares, 4 × 4 in (10 × 10cm). Spoon two mussels with their adhering sauce into the centre of each square. Gather up the corners and carefully twist and squeeze the pastry to hold. (Re-freeze any unused Filo pastry.) Brush each parcel liberally with more melted butter. Lift them onto a buttered baking sheet and bake in the centre of the oven for 10–12 minutes or until golden brown and crisp. Cool on a wire rack. As they are fragile, pack with plenty of tissue paper around them.

Fingers of white bread, spread with watercress butter and smoked halibut

6 slices white bread
4 oz (110 g) watercress butter, softened (see page 123)
6 oz (175 g) smoked halibut, thinly cut
6 small lemon wedges, cut from 1½ lemons, wrapped in muslin
milled black pepper

Spread the bread with the watercress. Butter to within a fraction of the crust edge. Lay over layers of the smoked halibut. Dredge lightly with milled pepper. Trim the edges and discard crusts. Cut into fingers or squares.

Pack flat, with waxed paper between. Pack lemon wedges for each guest to squeeze over at will.

To wrap lemon wedges, cut top and tail off each lemon. Cut in half, then in quarters. Pick out any major pips. Place each quarter-lemon in the centre of a 6 in (15 cm) square of clean butter muslin. Gather the corners together, twist hard and tuck in the 'tail' to secure.

Cherry tomatoes with soured cream and keta

12 even-sized cherry tomatoes (not too small, about 1 in (2.5 cm) in diameter)

up to ⅛ pt (75 ml) rich French dressing

milled black pepper or smidgin of cayenne pepper

¼ pt (150 ml) tub soured cream

2 oz (60 ml) glass Keta (red salmon caviar, *not* lumpfish roe)

Take the stalks off each tomato and stand them stalk-end down on a kitchen board. Using the tip of a small pointed knife, cut a 'lid' out of each about ¼ in (6 mm) down from the top. Shake out the seeds and water. Discard. Use the handle of a teaspoon to help do this if necessary. Spoon a modicum of French dressing onto each emptied tomato shell: add a smidgin of pepper, and leave to absorb for 30 minutes. Fill each shell with thick soured cream. Top with the lid. Transport the Keta in its jar and use a stainless-steel teaspoon to top each tomato with some of this just before eating.

Simple stuffed half eggs with tarragon

Creaming butter and fresh herbs make these perfect. If you have the patience, gulls' or quails' eggs are unusual when prepared this way, in which case allow 12 gulls' or 18 quails' eggs for 6 guests.

6 eggs, hard-boiled

3 oz (75 g) butter, softened

1 heaped tsp tarragon mustard or other mild French mustard

salt and freshly milled white pepper

1 tbsp parsley, freshly chopped

1 tbsp tarragon, freshly chopped

Halve the eggs lengthways and scoop out yolks. Mix the yolks, butter and mustard together. Press through a hair sieve. Season well. Mix in the parsley and tarragon. Pipe or fork into the halved whites.

Cold spiced chicken striplets

Marinade

2 tbsp good olive oil

1 tbsp strained Greek yoghurt

1 tsp mild French mustard

1 tbsp soy sauce

1 tbsp Amontillado sherry

1 tsp salt

1 tsp ground ginger

1 tsp ground mace

1 tsp milled pepper

1 tsp orange zest, fully grated

½ clove garlic, crushed

6 spring onions, trimmed and shredded

a little olive or soy oil for frying

Chicken

3 × 8 oz (225 g) boneless chicken breasts, skinned

In a large glass or china bowl, using a balloon whisk, mix together all the ingredients for the marinade. Cut each chicken breast into four diagonal strips. Mix into the marinade, and leave, covered with plastic film, for 4 hours or more.

Choose a large heavy-bottomed frying pan. Heat 2 tbsp oil until very hot and smoking. Working over a high heat all the time, quickly stir-fry the chicken striplets in 2 or 3 batches for no more than 2–3 minutes for each batch. The chicken must stay moist. Sprinkle each batch with their share of onions half a minute before they are cooked, allowing just enough time for the onions to wilt.

Remove each batch to a kitchen plate as it is done, allowing onions to adhere to the flesh.

Black figs with mascapone cheese and prosciutto

- **3 plump and ripe black figs, quartered**
- **12 × 1 in (2.5 cm) cubes Mascapone cheese**
- **12 thin slivers Prosciutto (Parma ham)**
- **¼ pt (150 ml) rich French dressing**

In a large glass bowl, turn and toss the figs in the dressing. On a kitchen board, lay out the slivers of ham and fold them sides to middles, lengthways. Place each fig, with a gobbet of cheese at one end. Roll up in the ham and secure with a wooden pick.

Individual beef tartares on rye discs

Tartare

- **2 tbsp olive or soy oil**
- **½ oz (15 g) butter**
- **1 × 2 oz (50 g) onion, skinned, thinly sliced**
- **2 small peppers (1 red, 1 yellow), seeded, pith 'ribs' cut away, thinly sliced**
- **12 oz (350 g) fillet steak, trimmed of all sinew and fat, minced**
- **strained juice of ½ lemon**
- **1 tsp mild French mustard**
- **1 tbsp very fresh parsley, finely chopped**
- **salt and milled pepper**

Bread

- **1 packet Danish Rye Bread (discs or slices) or other light rye bread of a similar firm texture**

Heat the oil and butter together in a pan until *almost* smoking. Add the sliced onions and peppers and cook over a medium to low heat until tender (about 20 minutes), stirring to prevent browning. Allow to cool completely. Drain retaining the oils. Chop finely with a knife.

In a bowl mix the peppers with the minced meat, lemon juice, mustard, parsley and the spare oils. Season well with salt and milled black pepper. Add a modicum more olive oil if the mixture doesn't look succulent (the beef absorbs quite a bit)

Pack into a container, cover first with plastic film then a lid. (If the surface of the tartare discolours slightly due to exposure to air over a prolonged time, this in no way impairs the flavour of the dish.)

To serve, spread on lightly buttered discs or fingers of rye bread or crisp biscuits. For extra luxury, a thin layer of Sevruga Caviar can be spread over each tartare as it is served.

Marrons glacés, Turkish Delight, marinated fingers of crystallized pineapple and melon

These can usually be purchased from any good Confectioners or Specialist food shop.

THE FORMAL PICNIC

I confess I have committed the cardinal sin. In 1981 I took a full-blown formal picnic to the lawns of Glyndebourne, complete with a centrepiece of scented white stephanotis and not one, but *two*, liveried butlers. I will never do it again. The embarrassment of being ogled at by fellow members of the audience as they brushed past the table en route for their own chosen covert was just too great for enjoyment. Mind you, much of the fault was self-inflicted, camp *had* been pitched on what I call the 'strawberry lawn', right by what I dub 'champagne corner'. It was impossible not to be seen, and hiding behind the programme was to no avail.

The site had been chosen, not by me you understand, but by my co-host, who perchanced also to be my business partner, Malcolm Livingston, and who swears he acquired his grand style whilst training in my establishment (as well as dining at my table, he adds, as if in some sort of self-defence). So, perhaps a modicum of the Smith style has rubbed off and I mustn't complain too loudly.

The presence of waiters, which inhibited my usually free-flowing conversation, is possibly the aspect to which I took most objection. But there are those to whom these things are no worry. In fact it is almost a natural lifestyle to them: eating out in smart restaurants; attending dinner parties in grand houses; having fashionable caterers take responsibility for entertaining in their own gracious homes; lunch on Concorde; evenings travelling on the Orient Express; then boxes at Ascot and strawberries and champagne at Wimbledon, in fact, going any place where the *arrivisti* and *haut monde* are to be seen.

The formal picnic with its attendant array is nothing if

Fresh Salmon and Smoked Salmon Mousse with Saffron Sauce and Keta

---

Cold Roast Spiced Fillet of Beef with Herb Garden Sauce

Aubergine Rings with Leeks and Plums

Baby Potato Salad with an Orange and Ginger Mint Dressing

Pineapple and Strawberry Salad with Drambuie

Cold Tarte Tatin with Soured Cream

not uninhibited exhibitionism. To my thinking it is simply a matter of arranging outside all that you would set out in your dining room at home. With care it is possible to take your finest china and crystal, silverware and napkins. Attendants are then necessary not least for security but also to hump the regalia from car to lawn or water's edge. For this type of picnic it is as well for everything to be transported in a separate vehicle and set up during the performance of the first act to avoid the otherwise ostentatious display during the preamble. It would also show some welcome discretion if your arrangements were made to one side of the campus, and not centre stage.

The British, perhaps boringly to some, tend towards understatement: this is not however reason enough for you to forego a lavish set-up if that is your style and you can carry it off with ease and aplomb. Many can and many do. Here's what I would serve.

Fresh salmon and smoked salmon mousse with saffron sauce and keta

Fish stock

3 lb (1.4 kg) headless white fish bones plus skin and bones from piece of salmon

2 sachets bouquet garni

1 tsp white peppercorns

1 medium onion, peeled, quartered, sliced

1 carrot, peeled, sliced

2 celery sticks, cut up

¼ pt (150 ml) dry white wine

No salt, yet

Salmon

12 oz (350 g) fresh Scotch smoked salmon to line mould

1 tsp salt

1 sachet gelatine

light olive or soy oil

Mousse mixture

1 lb (450 g) to yield 12 oz (350 g) salmon, weighed after boning

½ pt (275 ml) jellied stock (see below)

salt and milled white or black pepper

strained juice of ½ lemon

½ pt (275 ml) double cream (if possible not pasturised)

2 egg whites

First make the fish stock

Wash the fish bones under cold running water. Use a teaspoon to scrape away any blood running in the sack down the spine; discard this. Chop up the bone into manageable sizes for your pan. Put the bones and skin with all the other ingredients into a large 6–8 pt (3.4–4.5 l) pan. Cover with 3 pt (1.7 l) cold water. Bring to the boil very slowly. Boil at a low roll for 30–40 minutes. Cool. Strain into a basin.

Next cook the salmon

Put a piece of foil in the bottom of a pan just large enough to contain the salmon. Pour over enough fish stock just to cover. Season with 1 tsp of salt. Bring to the boil slowly; simmer for 2–3 minutes. Turn off the heat and leave to cool in the liquid.

Drain off the liquid and make up to ½ pt (275 ml) if necessary with some of the stock. In a small pan, bring this to the boil. Turn off the heat. Sprinkle over the entire sachet of gelatine and whisk until dissolved. Cool but do not allow to set.

Now to line the mould
Use a Le Creuset 9 × 4 in (23 × 10cm) terrine. Lightly brush bottom and sides with light olive or soy oil, *not* corn oil or sunflower seed oil: this has the wrong flavour. Cut a strip of greaseproof paper to fit the bottom and up the ends with a 1 in (2.5 cm) overlap at each end.

On a formica work surface lay out the pieces of smoked salmon. Cut and trim this appropriately to fit across the bottom and up the sides of the terrine or mould. Reserve enough pieces to lay on top of the mousse – *after* it has started to set, or they might sink into the mixture.
Note If, for whatever reason, you have too much mousse mixture, put this to set in little ramekins. The mixture should fill the terrine to within ¼–½ in (6–12 mm) of the top.

Then, make the mousse
Break the salmon into flakes: remove any bones and dark 'cream'. Make into a fine purée on a food processer fitted with the metal blade and using all the cold jellied stock. Scrape into a large bowl. Add extra seasoning and the lemon juice to taste.

Whip the cream, adding salt and pepper to taste, to soft peak (the tip of the peak should just fall back when drawn up with the whisk). Beat the 2 egg whites until standing in stiff peaks. Using a balloon whisk carefully and gradually incorporate the cream. Whisk well in one-third of the stiff whites. Cut and fold in the remainder. Pour into the lined mould. Refrigerate, covered, overnight.

Saffron sauce

1½ pt (850 ml) fish stock

¼ pt (150 ml) dry white vermouth

1 sachet saffron threads

1 tbsp whisky

⅓ pt (200 ml) unpasturized doubled cream

salt to taste

Garnish

1 oz (25 g) jar well chilled Keta (red salmon caviar *not* lumpfish roe) radicchio or frisée leaves

In a stainless or enamel pan, bring the stock and vermouth to a rolling boil and reduce to about ¼ pt (150 ml) of viscous-looking fish glaze. Strain into a clean pan. Add the saffron and let this infuse until bright yellow. Add the whisky and cream and bubble gently for 2–3 minutes, stirring from time to time. Cool. Strain into a clean basin, cover with plastic film and refrigerate until ready to serve.

To serve the mousse
Have ready a flat platter or dish large enough to contain the mousse. Run an oiled palette knife or table knife very carefully round the sides of the mould. Place the platter over the top and invert the two. If there is an air lock, press the palette knife down the end and ease the mousse from the side of the mould until this is released.
(a) Either serve the mousse whole and the sauce separately, having very carefully stirred the Keta into the sauce, or
(b) Have waiting in the refrigerator, the appropriate number of chilled 8 in (20 cm) fish or pudding plates.

When ready to serve the mousse, lay these out on a table. Arrange a neat radicchio or frisée leaf to one side of the plate. Spoon a pool of sauce onto the plate ready to receive a slice of the mousse.
(c) Take a serrated knife (not saw-toothed) Run this under hot water and carefully cut the mousse into 3/4 in (2 cm) slices; use a fish slice to support each slice of mousse as you cut it to prevent it breaking and to 'catch' the slice.

Lift the mousse on the slice, and, using the knife ease it onto the plate. Use a teaspoon to scatter portions of the Keta onto the sauce.

Roast spiced fillet of beef with herb garden sauce

1 whole fillet of beef, trimmed, tied and weighing approx 2 lb (900 g)

Basting mixture

4 oz (110 g) butter, softened

1 small clove of garlic, crushed

2 tsp salt (or less)

2 tsp milled black pepper

1 heaped tsp English mustard powder

1 heaped tsp ground ginger

2 tbsp very finely snipped chives

Plus

4 tsp whole grain mustard mixed with 2 tsp brown sugar

Sauce

⅓ pt (200 ml) olive oil

1 fl oz (30 ml) lemon juice

1 meat stock cube dissolved in ½ cup boiling water, then cooled

2 teacups well packed with fresh parsley, picked, stalks discarded

1 in (2.5 cm) bunch of chives, roughly chopped

1 tsp rubbed fresh or dried thyme

1 teacup fresh basil leaves, lightly packed

2–3 dashes Tabasco sauce

salt and pepper if necessary

You may find it easier to handle if you purchase two 1½–2 lb (700–900 g) fillets of beef. Have your butcher trim off all fat and sinew, and tie it at 1 in (2.5 cm) intervals with string. Take a fork and mash together on a plate all ingredients for the basting mixture. Using a small, sharp, pointed knife, plunge this deep into the flesh at 1 in (2.5 cm) intervals or thereabouts (in fact, between the string ties). Press the aperture open and push in a small nugget of the basting mixture. Withdraw the knife. Spread the remaining mixture all over the fillet. Spread over the top only a cushion of the whole-grain mustard and sugar.

Preheat the oven to 475°F (240°C) Reg 9. Stand the fillet(s) on a wire roasting rack in a roasting tin and roast the meat at this very high temperature for 20 minutes. Then reduce the temperature to 425°F (220°C) Reg 7 for a further 20 minutes for rare cooked beef. Allow longer if you want the fillet more done. It doesn't matter if the top coating gets over-browned.

Take the meat from the oven. Allow to cool completely. Only refrigerate the meat if absolutely necessary, and then in a plastic bag loosely tied. Transport the fillet(s) whole, carving in ¼ in (6 mm) thick slivers on site, as it were, each sliver with a teaspoon of the rich herb sauce.

To make the sauce put all the ingredients into a blender and blend to a fine emulsion. Shake or stir well before serving.

Aubergine rings with leeks and plums

2 'straight' aubergines

Topping

6 young leeks, washed, diced

6 ripe but still firm Victoria plums, halved, pitted

olive or soy oil for frying

1 clove garlic, crushed

salt and milled pepper

1 tsp ground mace

1 tsp ground coriander

Garnish

2 tbsp freshly chopped parsley, basil, or other green herbs

Top and tail the aubergines by cutting ½ in (1.2 cm) off each end and discarding the two pieces. Cut each aubergine into 8 evenly thick rings.

Bring to the boil a large pan of salted water. Poach the aubergines in two batches until *almost* transparent through (2–3 minutes). Remove them with a draining spoon first to a colander, then to layers of absorbent kitchen paper to absorb excess moisture, and cool completely.

To make the topping, dice the leeks. Dice the pitted plums.

Heat 2 tbsp of olive or soy oil in a large pan. Add the leeks, plums and garlic. Season with the salt, mace and coriander. Cover with a lid and simmer over a low heat until all is soft. Allow to cool.

To fry the aubergines, heat 3–4 tbsp oil in a large frying pan until well smoking. Fry the aubergine rings in batches until well browned on both sides, adding more oil if needed. Remove the rings as they are ready to a serving dish, arranging them in one layer. Leave to cool. Apportion the filling to each ring. Sprinkle liberally with your chosen herb just before packing.

Serves 8

Note By poaching the aubergines you reduce the amount of oil you would normally expect to use when frying them.

Baby potato salad with an orange and ginger mint dressing

Dressing

3 tbsp olive oil

strained juice of ½ orange

1 tsp orange zest, finely grated

2 tsp caster sugar

½ clove garlic, crushed

1 tsp ground ginger

24 or more washed ginger mint leaves, torn

salt (little)

Salad

2 lb (900 g) graded baby new potatoes

chicken stock for cooking

Shake all the dressing ingredients, *except* the ginger mint, in a screw-top jar to emulsify. Cook the potatoes in the chicken stock, leaving them slightly firm to the tooth. Drain, reserving the stock for another use.

Toss the potatoes whilst still hot in the dressing. Cool. Chill. Mix in the ginger mint leaves just before packing.

Pineapple and strawberry salad with Drambuie

1 lb (450 g) strawberries

1 small pineapple

2 oz (50 g) caster sugar

juice of 1 lemon

4 fl oz (110 ml) Drambuie

Quarter the strawberries. Peel and core the pineapple. Cut into ½ in (1.2 cm) thick strips and then into ½ in (1.2 cm) bits. Dredge with caster sugar. Toss the pineapple and strawberries in the juice and liqueur. Chill well.

Serves 6–8

Cold tarte tatin with soured cream

Pastry

6 oz (175 g) self-raising flour

4 oz (110 g) unsalted butter

2 tsp icing sugar

pinch of salt

1 egg beaten with 1 tbsp cold water

cream or sour cream for serving

Filling

5 large dessert apples

squeeze lemon juice

4 oz (110 g) unsalted butter, softened

6 oz (175 g) caster sugar

Make up the pastry and leave in a cool place to rest for 30 minutes. Then roll it out in one piece to make a lid to fit your dish. Take a tin or metal seamless dish 8–9 in (20–23 cm) in diameter. Peel, core and slice the apples into water with a squeeze of lemon juice added to prevent discoloration. Spread the softened butter over the entire base of the tin. Cover with a layer of sugar, using it all. Drain and pat dry the apples and arrange over the butter and sugar.

Cover with lid of pastry as you would do for an ordinary pie, but omitting the pastry edges. Bake in a preheated oven at 425°F (220°C) Reg 7 for 45 minutes. If, after 20 minutes, the pastry is nearly burning, lower the temperature a notch, but remember the pastry ought to be very brown and crisp. Place a serving dish over the finished *tarte* and invert the two. The finished result should be a sticky caramel apple mixture on top of the crisp pastry. Serve with chilled cream or sour cream.

Serves 6–8

Note If you have a thin-bottomed tin and an Aga, success should be immediate. If not, you might discover that the marriage of your particular mould and your particular oven doesn't produce a rich, dark, sticky caramel. In this case, make a fudge with the butter and sugar in a pan on top of the stove, taking the mixture to almost caramel stage before pouring it into a tin and topping with the sliced apples and pastry lid.

A COLD WEATHER PICNIC

Even the optimists have to agree that the gods do not always look kindly on picnickers at Glyndebourne, and even if the weather during the day has been good, eating *alfresco* at seven o'clock in the evening at the end of May can be a chilly affair.

There are a variety of ways you can attempt to get the better of these gods (although why they should be so unkind to those in the innocent pursuit of picnicking between bouts of glorious music is unclear). The first and obvious tip is to come equipped with many layers of extra clothing. By all means sit in the opera house in your diaphanous pink number but you should at the very least have brought a shawl, a cloak and, in really appalling weather, a Barbour to see you through the interval. It is extremely difficult to enjoy yourself, however determined, if you are cold.

Most people, when faced with hopelessly inclement weather on a planned picnic day, will decide to abandon ship and eat inside. This is easier said than done at Glyndebourne when the entire outing has been organized since February. So you try to book a table in the restaurant; full. You try to get a table in the marquee; too late, full. You try Mildmay Hall; full. What do you do? You are British, you are brave, you stiffen your upper lip, put on your wellies and make for the gardens, persuading yourself that it is 'only a shower' and that the wind always drops in the evening. Now this scenario could be extremely sad were it not for one thing – you have had the foresight to bring a picnic of comforting hot food and drink, to the enormous envy of those around you who only have iced champagne.

Start the evening with mulled wine or punch or, if you haven't enough thermos flasks for soup, coffee and punch,

Hot Tomato and Fennel Soup

Sauté of Veal with Mushrooms, Coriander, Cream and Cashews
New Potatoes
Mixed Green Salad

Chocolate Mousse in Orange Pastry Crust

bring some brandy to put in the coffee at the end of the meal – this wonderfully warming potion is sold in the intervals at the Santa Fe Opera in New Mexico. There at 6000 ft (1829 m) above sea level the evenings are sharp and bright. Although the opera house is partially covered the bars are not, so the audience, wrapped up warm against the chill, sip the steaming intoxicating coffee whilst watching the huge expanse of the New Mexican skyline burst into flames as the sun sets.

It must be said before going further that this picnic is not suitable for anyone who has much more than an hour's journey to Glyndebourne, as the food does not remain satisfactorily hot for more than three to four hours. All these recipes taste very good warm, rather than piping hot, but if you want the benefit of a warming meal you will need to eat them as hot as possible.

Go, then, to your nearest hardware store and buy up all their thermos flasks. You must then find a deep basket to pack them into. For four people you will need one large or two medium flasks for soup, two large food jars (you can easily buy very inexpensive plastic rather than glass insulated food flasks), one for the meat and one for the potatoes and a pouring thermos jug for the coffee. Add to this another thermos jug for the mulled wine and you will see why you may attract strange glances from rival picnickers. Don't be put off – it will be worth it.

Hot tomato and fennel soup

However delicious green vegetable soups are at home in the summer, they are not suitable candidates for the thermos flask: what was fresh and green when put in the flask will look sad and brownish when poured out several hours later. It is best, therefore, to stick to soups that retain their colour and freshness. Tomato is ideal for this.

2 small bulbs fennel, or 1 large bulb

2 tbsp olive oil

1 lb (450 g) fresh ripe tomatoes

2 cloves garlic

½ pt (275 ml) V8 juice or tomato juice

grated rind of ½ lemon

salt and pepper

½ tsp white sugar

½ pt (275 ml) chicken stock

1 tbsp fresh dill, chopped

2 tbsp dry Italian or French Vermouth (optional)

Wash and chop the fennel. Heat the oil in a thick pan, add the fennel and cook over a gentle heat for 10 minutes until soft but not browned, stirring occasionally. Meanwhile peel the tomatoes by plunging them for a minute in boiling water. Roughly chop them. Crush the garlic into the fennel,

A COLD WEATHER PICNIC

stir round and cook for 1 minute then add the tomatoes, V8 juice, lemon rind, salt, pepper, sugar and chicken stock. Bring to the boil and simmer for 5 minutes. Take off the heat and liquidize or process the soup. Clean the pan and pour it back, bringing to boiling point again, add the dill and the Vermouth, test for seasoning and add a little more stock if it is too thick for your taste (much depends on how watery the tomatoes are). When fully heated through, put into a thermos flask previously heated with boiling water.

Sauté of veal with mushrooms, coriander, cream and cashews

This is light, creamy and very easy to make and manages to combine elegance with comfort.

1 tbsp light oil

3 oz (75 g) cashew nuts

1 oz (25 g) butter plus 1 tbsp oil

1 lb (450 g) lean veal, not necessarily escalopes, cut into thin strips about 1½ in (4 cm) long and ½ in (1.2 cm) wide.

½ large or 1 small red pepper, finely sliced

6 oz (175 g) mushrooms, thinly sliced

1 tsp coriander seeds, lightly crushed

salt

black pepper, freshly ground

1 dsp flour

3 fl oz (85 ml) white wine

½ pt (275 ml) single cream

juice of 1 lemon

Heat 1 tbsp oil in a small heavy-bottomed pan, add the cashew nuts and sauté until browned. Drain on kitchen paper and set aside. Heat the remaining oil and butter in a large frying pan or sauté pan and sauté the veal over a high flame until browned. Turn down the heat and add the red peppers, cook for a few minutes and add the mushrooms, stirring all the time, then the crushed coriander seeds, salt and freshly ground black pepper. Turn up the heat again and cook until the liquid made by the mushrooms has nearly evaporated, then sprinkle on the flour. Stir well, add the wine stirring constantly whilst it thickens, scraping all the crunchy bits off the bottom of the pan. Turn the flame down again, add salt and pepper, then the cream and lemon juice and let it bubble for a couple more minutes. Check for seasoning then pour straight away into a thermos food jar which has been pre-heated with boiling water. Cover and leave for the picnic as soon as possible.

Alternatively, you can cook this in advance (but no more than the morning of the day on which you intend to eat it) then heat it through thoroughly with a lid on the pan before pouring it into the heated thermos. Take the cashews in a separate pot and sprinkle some on top of each serving at the picnic – if you put them in the meat they will soften and lose that magical roasted nut flavour.

New potatoes

1 lb (450 g) very small English or Jersey new potatoes of uniform size

Wash the potatoes but do not peel them. Cook them in lightly salted boiling water for about 8 minutes or until tender (this obviously depends on the size). Drain and put immediately into a pre-heated insulated food jar.

Really good small new potatoes like this need no embellishments – no butter, no oil – and they will provide the perfect foil to the creamy richness of the veal. As you can clean them in advance, the final cooking, draining and placing in the thermos can be done in your Glyndebourne outfit just before leaving. There will be no danger of getting messy.

Mixed green salad

A simple mixed green salad is the other accompaniment to the main course of this picnic. Choose what you like in the way of greenery – this is one of my favourite combinations.

1 bunch fresh dark green watercress

1 fat stick chicory

1 plump-hearted English cabbage or cos lettuce

Pick over the watercress and discard the stalks and any yellowing leaves. Put in a bag or plastic box. Take apart the chicory and chop into 1 in (2.5 cm) long pieces. Add to the watercress. Wash the lettuce, dry carefully, tear into manageable pieces, taking out the hard stalks and add to the other greenery. Add some chopped fresh herbs if you like, cover and pack into the picnic box or basket.

Take a light vinaigrette dressing with you in a jar (see page 101).

Chocolate mousse in orange pastry crust

I always find chocolate particularly warming and comforting. This is a delicious pudding, the sort guests refuse at first on the grounds that it is bad for their waistlines and then return for second helpings.

Pastry

4 oz (110 g) flour

grated rind of 1 orange

2 oz (50 g) icing sugar

3 oz (75 g) butter

½ egg yolk

about 1 tbsp freshly squeezed orange juice

Heat the oven to 400°F (200°C) Reg 6. Sift the flour, orange rind and icing sugar into a bowl, cut the butter up into it and rub together until the mixture resembles fine breadcrumbs. Add the egg yolk and enough orange juice to form a soft dough (about 1 tbsp). Roll the dough out a little and put it in a 7–8 in (18–20 cm) flan tin with removeable base; it will be rather sticky to roll out so use plenty of flour and when you have got it in the tin press it up the sides and over the base until it is evenly and thinly distributed. The crust should be thin so if you have some pastry left over don't worry. Tidy up the edges and put in the refrigerator for at least 30 minutes.

Filling

3 eggs

1 tbsp caster sugar

4 oz (110 g) plain bitter cooking chocolate

1 tbsp orange juice or orange liqueur (Grand Marnier, Cointreau or Curaçao)

1½ oz (40 g) butter

Separate the eggs and add the sugar to the yolks in a basin. Beat well with a rotary whisk until pale, fluffy and slightly thickened. Break the chocolate into a small saucepan and add the orange juice or liqueur and melt over a low flame until smooth. Take off the heat and add the butter a little at a time until incorporated in the chocolate. If it does not readily melt, put it back on the heat. Leave to cool slightly then whisk into the egg yolk and sugar mixture. Beat the egg whites until they stand in soft peaks and fold carefully into the chocolate mixture with a metal spoon. Pour into the chilled pastry case and bake in the centre of the oven for 30 minutes or until well risen and just set in the centre. Leave to cool – it will sink a little, but don't worry.

When cool sprinkle with icing sugar and it is ready to pack for the picnic. Take some lightly whipped cream separately. If you like, a spoonful of raspberries would be delicious with this pudding.

THE NO-COOKING PICNIC

Picture this scenario. Your uncle, who is a most important something in the City, rings you on Monday night to say that he and your Aunt feel like a little holiday, so would you like a couple of tickets for Glyndebourne tomorrow? No, they haven't a table booked in the restaurant, Monica always gets Justin de Blanc to produce something. He very much hopes you will enjoy it – he can't remember which opera it is.

You are thrilled because you love opera, but, being a struggling poet you are penniless and can't cook – not, of course, that that is a *sine qua non*. You invite Samantha, a rather grand drama student whom you have been longing to impress. She also is thrilled, particularly as you assure her you will take care of *everything*, yes, of course including the picnic. Help! What do you do?

There are basically two ways of tackling this. Either you go to the best delicatessen you know and buy as many goodies as you fancy and can afford, or you try the slightly more dangerous but much more enjoyable ploy of kidding Samantha into believing you are an inspired cook. Either way, you first go to the Post Office and get out your savings. The secret will be to plan your meal with great care so that each separate dish and course complements the others perfectly – in that way you will appear to *understand* food, and if you have not actually cooked it you can always say that you were working to a deadline for your latest article in *Poetry Monthly*.

If you choose to go to Marks and Spencer or a delicatessen, don't be tempted to buy lots of little pots of

Smoked Salmon with Rose Peppercorns and Oil
Brown Bread and Butter

Plate of Cold Roast Beef
or Italian Charcuterie
New Potatoes with Horseradish Mayonnaise
Watercress

Strawberries and Cream
Marrons Glacés
Cheese and Biscuits

---

or

Paté de Foie Gras Truffé

Smoked Trout with Cucumber Salad
New Potatoes (as above)

Peaches in White Wine
Best 'Home-made' Truffles you can buy
Cheese and Biscuits

different mixed salads – they may look appetizing in the shop but when you get them on your plate they will all taste exactly the same with the same mass-produced vinaigrette – and Samantha will *know*. The same goes for the fish pâtés, taramasalata and meat pâtés, unless you have tried them before and you know they are genuinely home-made. The best thing is to go for food that has to be bought and can't reasonably be home-made, like Italian charcuterie, and very simple things that just need poaching or boiling and are then ready to eat.

You will, I hope, go to the trouble of borrowing an attractive picnic basket from your Mama or landlady together with tablecloth and napkins. Plenty of well chosen wine, Perrier water and a fresh lime to slice in the water will all help to persuade Samantha that, for a poet, you do produce a marvellous picnic.

Even if you cannot identify with the scenario in the introduction to this chapter there may well be times when you simply cannot give the time to buying and cooking for a Glyndebourne picnic but nevertheless wish to have one rather than go to the expense of getting someone else to do it, or eating in the restaurant.

Here are two menus. They are, as you can see, very straightforward and simple; more elaborate mass-produced food, even from the grandest shops, very often tastes of monosodium glutamate and not much else.

Smoked salmon with rose peppercorns and oil

This is a delectable Italian way of serving Smoked Salmon.

smoked salmon

1 pot rose peppercorns packed in brine (available from really good delicatessens – if you *really* can't find them, use green peppercorns

best quality olive oil

lemon

Spread the smoked salmon out on the plates. Sprinkle 1 tsp of the peppercorns over it, then 1 tbsp of best olive oil. A squeeze of lemon juice adds the finishing touch if you like (I prefer it without).

Cold roast beef

Go to a shop where you know you can get really rare roast beef and get them to cut as many slices as you want. Serve them with good quality horseradish and/or mustard, and, if you can rise to it, the potato salad in the following recipe.

Italian charcuterie

Alternatively, you can go to a specialist Italian delicatessen and buy a selection of their delicious cold meats. Try the Salami Milanese, which is quite big in diameter, coarse and garlicky; Parma Ham or Bressaiolo, the cured beef cut in very thin slices which you serve with black pepper and olive oil. If serving Italian meat buy some marinated artichoke hearts to go with it, or large mild olives.

New potatoes with horseradish mayonnaise

It should not be beyond the wit of even the most fervent non-cook to boil a few new potatoes. I suggest these should be bought at Marks and Spencer, or somewhere similar, as there will be no need to do any preparation except rinse them under the tap. Use 1 lb (450 g) potatoes and they should be of uniform size, or just about, otherwise some will overcook, whilst others will undercook. Boil them in 4 in (10 cm) water into which you have put 1 tsp salt for 8 minutes, or until tender when pierced with a thin sharp knife. Drain in a sieve or colander and leave to cool. You can then coat them in a sauce made of ½ pt (275 ml) bought mayonnaise, 1–2 tbsp horseradish relish and 2 tbsp milk, all mixed together. Or a dressing of 1 tsp Dijon mustard, 1 tsp wine vinegar, 5 tbsp olive oil, ½ tsp salt and ½ tsp black pepper all mixed together.

Watercress

For greenery take three bunches of fresh dark green watercress and spend some time picking it over, removing the thick, hairy stalks and keeping only the very best of the thinner stalks and luscious leaves. Put them on a dish and carefully lay the beef on top. Charcuterie looks better on a plate by itself so put the watercress in a separate white china or wooden bowl.

Strawberries and cream

Choose shiny fresh strawberries, preferably from a fruit farm. If you buy them in punnets make sure there aren't any mouldy ones lurking under the good-looking ones on top. Hull the strawberries before leaving home and only wipe them if very muddy. Don't wash them as they are bound to go mushy in an airtight container if wet. An airtight box *is* important if the fruit is to be transported in a modern cool-box or picnic bag as the flavour of strawberries tends to pervade everything – including mayonnaise if shut in with other food.

Always serve caster sugar, rather than granulated, and real Jersey cream rather than the white supermarket variety.

Cheese and biscuits

Many people feel slightly cheated if they are not offered cheese at the end of a meal, but it can be untidy and difficult to serve at a picnic. Here are some ways of getting round this problem. Don't be too ambitious – instead of providing a large cheeseboard offer only two very carefully chosen cheeses. Perhaps one hard and one soft, or one goat's cheese and one blue cheese.

It is worth taking trouble to find unusual cheeses so go if possible to a specialist cheese shop rather than your usual supermarket. Before leaving for the opera rewrap the cheeses individually in foil rather than Clingfilm which tends to make cheese sweat in hot weather and bring a small board or plate to serve them off together with a mixture of biscuits in an airtight container. With our present preoccupations about diet I never now provide butter to eat with cheese, but if you must, bring it in a little airtight pot or deep dish with a lid. Quite high up the list of regular picnic disasters is rather warm soft butter coating the bottoms of dishes in the picnic hamper, which is then smeared over the hostess's dress.

Pâté de foie gras truffé

For 1 lb (450 g) of really fine pâté you can pay as much as for a Glyndebourne ticket, so you obviously get what you pay for. Serve the pâté on very plain toasts (you can get fine Melba toast in packets now), crispbread or biscuits. You should also serve a fine wine with it.

Smoked trout with cucumber salad

Of all the smoked fish on the market this is, to my mind, the nicest. It hasn't the cloying richness of a smoked mackerel or the oiliness of eel.

1 small smoked trout per person

½ cucumber

4 oz (110 g) strawberries

fresh dill for garnish

Slice the cucumber as thinly as you possibly can and line the bottom of a flat dish with the pieces overlapping like fish scales. Lay the fish on top and put more slices on the fish. Hull the strawberries and cut them in quarters and scatter them over the fish and the cucumber, or put them in artistic patterns if you prefer. Do likewise with the dill. Serve it with ½ pt (275 ml) bought mayonnaise into which you have incorporated 2 tbsp horseradish relish.

The only accompaniment to this need be some good-quality wholemeal bread, or the potato salad in the previous recipe (if you use the horseradish mayonnaise on the potatoes, you obviously will not need it with the fish as well).

Peaches in white wine

You will have brought some good white wine to drink with the fish. Make sure you bring enough to keep drinking throughout the pudding and simply peel some very good ripe peaches into your glass of wine. Leave for a few minutes, then spoon out and eat. A wonderful and rather sensuous pudding for which you will need to protect your shirtfront.

Finish the meal with the most expensive 'home-made' chocolate truffles you can buy and good black coffee.

A FRENCH PICNIC

When I think of a French picnic I am always reminded of Elizabeth David's description of one she had when staying in Marseille with friends. They made a plan to meet another party of friends at a nearby bay, each with their own picnics. The second party (who were American) turned up with a superbly elaborate affair involving cutlets and potatoes to cook over a fire while Mrs David and her party had gone to the local market and had a marvellous time choosing olives, cheese, anchovies, salami, pâtés and bread – a typical French picnic. When the time came for lunch, however, and the contrasting picnics were laid out, it became obvious how inferior the French one was. No ice, no butter, no tablecloths, no coffee. Even the food seemed dull and wilted in its oily bits of paper compared with the jauntily sizzling cutlets in the frying pan.

The lesson to learn from this sad tale is that the inferiority of the French picnic had nothing at all to do with the quality of the food. Most of us know how delicious that French picnic food is, bought perhaps early in the morning in the market in Dieppe, or St Malo or wherever you get off the boat. No, the problem was that Mrs David's party were too impulsive. Put it down to the sun, the sea and the heady scent of wild thyme, but they didn't think to pack all the little extras that the American party so clearly demonstrated were essential to a good picnic. Just a large flat white dish on which to arrange the dappled pink salami, shiny olives and crumbly white goat's cheese; that and a basket for the bread would have saved their embarrassment.

At Glyndebourne people tend to go to a lot of trouble with the presentation of their picnics and less trouble over what they are going to eat – quite the reverse of Mrs David and her friends. Here is a French picnic which tries to combine the two, although the food is not bought from a French market at dawn. It would be possible, though – the Dieppe-Newhaven ferry gets in at mid-day having left Dieppe at 07.00, and Newhaven is twenty minutes from Glyndebourne.

Rabbit Pâté with Mushrooms and Green Peppercorns

Leek and Goat's Cheese Tart
Tomato and Onion Salad
Frisée aux Fines Herbes

Orange and Strawberry Crème Brûlée

Rabbit pâté with mushrooms and green peppercorns

This is a typical fairly substantial French pâté, given added elegance by the addition of the peppercorns.

- **8 oz (225 g) belly of pork**
- **8 oz (225 g) boned rabbit meat**
- **8 oz (225 g) stewing veal**
- **4 oz (110 g) hard back pork fat**
- **8 rashers streaky smoked bacon**
- **8 oz (225 g) chopped onion**
- **4 plump cloves garlic, crushed**
- **½ tsp salt**
- **1 tsp ground black pepper**
- **1½ tsp green peppercorns (use the type packed in brine, not the dried variety)**
- **1 tbsp dried or fresh chopped thyme**
- **1 small wineglass white wine**
- **2 fl oz (60 ml) cooking brandy**

Mushrooms

- **2 oz (50 g) butter**
- **6 oz (175 g) flat-capped mushrooms**
- **grated rind of 1 lemon**
- **2 cloves garlic**
- **salt and pepper**
- **1 tbsp chopped parsley**

Grind all of the meat and the back fat (not the bacon) in small batches in the food processor until it is finely chopped but not pulverized and put it in a basin. Add the chopped onion, the garlic, salt, pepper, green peppercorns, thyme, wine and brandy. Mix all together and leave in a cool place to marinate for at least two hours.

To prepare the mushrooms, melt the butter in a frying pan and add the mushrooms and all the other ingredients except the parsley. Cook for a few minutes until the mushrooms are cooked and all the liquid has been absorbed, add the parsley, take off the flame and set aside.

Line a 2 pt (1.2 l) loaf tin or terrine, or two 1 pt (575 ml) terrines or tins with the bacon. Pack the meat mixture in until halfway up then add a layer of mushrooms then fill up with the rest of the meat mixture. If you have any over, put it in a separate little pot to cook. Cover the tins or terrines in a double layer of foil, then the lids if they have them and place in a baking tin with water halfway up their sides. Cook in a slow oven (300°F/150°C/Reg 2) for 3 hours. Leave to rest for about 10 minutes then remove the lids and place weights on top of the foil. Place in a cool place until cold, then in the fridge overnight. When ready to pack for the picnic, remove the weights and the foil and turn the pâté out onto a plate. Wrap in fresh foil, or slice first then wrap in foil and pack in an insulated picnic bag.

Leek and goat's cheese tart

This bears little resemblance to the ubiquitous quiche, stodgy and soggy, that graces the counters of delicatessens everywhere. This is unusual and utterly delicious. Try to cook it on the morning of the picnic and leave in a coolish place, but not the fridge, before putting it in the picnic basket. For a 9 in (23 cm) removable-bottomed flan tin you will need:

Pastry

- **2 oz (50 g) butter**
- **2 oz (50 g) blended cooking fat or lard**
- **8 oz (225 g) flour**
- **1 egg yolk**
- **water**

Filling

- **12 oz (350g) small tender leeks**
- **2 oz (50 g) butter**
- **6 oz (175 g) goat's cheese with rind removed**
- **1 clove garlic**
- **1 tsp Dijon mustard**
- **¼ tsp curry powder**
- **1 large egg**
- **6 fl oz (170 ml) double cream**
- **salt and freshly ground black pepper**
- **1 tbsp fresh breadcrumbs**

Rub the fats into the flour. Add the egg yolk and enough water (1–2 tbsp) to make a firmish dough. Form into a ball, wrap up and put in the fridge to rest for at least 30 minutes. When you are ready, roll out the pastry and line a flan tin or white china flan dish. Neaten the edges and bake blind by putting greaseproof paper and dried beans in the pastry case and baking in a fairly hot oven (425°F/220°C/Reg 7). Remove the paper and beans after 10 minutes and continue cooking until dry and golden brown (another 5 minutes). Cool.

Meanwhile slice the leeks into ¼ in (6 mm) rounds. Melt the butter in a heavy-bottomed pan, add the leeks and cook gently, making sure they don't even brown for 15 minutes or until soft. Tip into the pastry case and distribute evenly. Crumble all but 1 tbsp of the goat's cheese onto the leeks.

Crush the garlic into a bowl. Add the mustard, the curry powder and the egg and mix well. Add the cream and beat well. Season. Pour the custard onto the leeks. Sprinkle the top with the remaining goat's cheese and the breadcrumbs and bake in the centre of a moderate oven (400°F/200°C/Reg 6) until puffed up and golden brown (about 25–30 minutes) Leave to cool.

Tomato and onion salad

This is a very good salad; a clean simple foil to the richness of the quiche.

12 oz (350 g) ripe fresh tomatoes

1 small sweet onion

1 small green chilli

salt and pepper

sprinkling of white or red wine vinegar

1 tbsp olive oil

Slice the tomatoes and put them in a dish. Slice the onion incredibly finely: almost transparent wafer-thin circles are what you are after. Sprinkle them over the tomatoes. Do the same with the chilli (as much as you wish), very, very finely sliced. Sprinkle this on the tomatoes. Grind the salt and pepper, sprinkle the vinegar and pour over the oil. Cover and pack into the picnic basket.

Frisée aux fines herbes

Frisée, Escarole and other mixed-salad greens would go well with this picnic. Buy a selection from your greengrocer, wash it, dry it and put it in a plastic bag with 1 tbsp freshly chopped herbs. Take the following vinaigrette dressing separately in a firmly closed container.

1 tsp Dijon mustard

½ tsp salt

½ tsp black pepper, freshly ground

2 tbsp Tarragon vinegar

10 tbsp good quality olive oil

Put the mustard, salt and pepper in a cup, add the vinegar and stir well. Add the oil and stir vigorously until mixed.

Orange and strawberry crème brûlée

This is a classic *crème brûlée* with a difference – hidden in the bottom of the dish are fresh strawberries.

8 oz (225 g) strawberries

6 egg yolks

1½ oz (40 g) caster sugar

grated rind of ½ orange

1½ pt (850 ml) double cream

1 vanilla pod

extra sugar

Hull the strawberries, slice them in half and put them in the bottom of six ramekins. Beat the egg yolks with the sugar and the orange rind until light and fluffy, and the mixture runs in ribbons off the spoon. Heat the cream gently in a heavy-bottomed pan with the vanilla pod. Wait until it is hot but not quite boiling and pour it in a steady stream onto the egg yolks stirring all the time. Put in a double saucepan and cook gently until it thickens. Don't let it get too hot or the eggs will scramble. Pour onto the fruit in the ramekins and place in the top of the fridge.

Sprinkle an even layer of caster sugar on top of each pudding and brown under a very hot grill until caramelized. Leave to cool again. Cover and pack carefully.

THE CHINESE 'STEAMBOAT' PICNIC

For their international tour in 1986, Glyndebourne got its very complex act together and went to Hong Kong (near enough to China as not to signify), where they performed to great acclaim Mozart's 'Don Giovanni' and Britten's 'A Midsummer Night's Dream' in front of a sophisticated international audience.

An opera with a Chinese motif has never been given at Glyndebourne, however

To the amateur or lay person this is puzzling, for surely Puccini's 'Butterfly' seems a natural choice? I'm told by my old friend Geoffrey Parsons – himself no slouch at preparing a picnic in his days there as *répétiteur* – that the kind of singing required would not be of the right scale for the house; yet to me 'La Bohème' seems similar in stature and that was produced there. Moreover, 'Turandot' appears no less grand than say 'Carmen' or 'Der Rosenkavalier', and Glyndebourne designers are past-masters at creating illusions of grandeur, *vide* 'Poppea', 'Onegin' and (my favourite sets) 'Macbeth' – but there has not yet been a production of this Puccini masterpiece. Maybe I'll have to have my proposed Chinese picnic without the strains of an appropriate opera wafting over the evening air from the Green Room.

A Chinese 'steamboat' would fit into the scheme of things admirably: it may raise an eyebrow from those devotees of the establishment who find change difficult to take and innovation suspect, if not undesirable. Yet the 'steamboat' is a gentle thing, as gentle as 'Butterfly' herself,and I can just imagine her overseeing such a party. It is a method of cooking

Sesame Vinegar Dip
Fresh Chilli Dip

Won Ton (Chinese Dumplings)

Beef Fillet
Pork Fillet
Chicken Breast
Prawns
Squid
Broccoli Spears
Spinach Leaves
Asparagus
Special Chicken Stock

Fresh Lychees
Compôte of Kumquats
Jar of Stem Ginger

which fits well with the picnic notion of our book. You will perforce have to invest in a good piece of apparatus, preferably one with a neat bottled gas burner.

For the rest, the delicious slivers of meat, fish and poultry destined for this delicate way of eating are prepared at home by the deft use of a sharp knife and packed into chilled containers ready to be cooked and enjoyed during the interval.

I was first introduced to *Cheng Loong*, or Steamboat, by Tam Cheong, a talented young Chinese designer friend. He uses this intimate idea of serving food when entertaining more than a dozen people informally in his home, where he arranges two or three tables of four or more and leaves his guests to their own devices to dip and catch delicious morsels of raw meat, fish and vegetables in a steaming boat of boiling rich chicken stock.

Each guest retrieves his food by means of an individual wire-mesh scoop held in the one hand, and a pair of chopsticks in the other with which to pick up and dip his chosen piece into a mild or hot relish before eating it. The potential of *Cheng Loong* as an outside event is hitherto uncharted, and maybe you will make history and be the first to initiate the idea at Glyndebourne!

In place of the traditional but now out-moded charcoal brazier, I suggest you take along a liquid gas burner and an 8–10 pt (4.5–5.5 l) brightly coloured pan or casserole. The stock can be transported and re-decanted when cool again into a plastic container.

It is also a good idea to take a large plastic tray or board to form a safe platform for all this, and a wind-shield might also be a good idea. The special equipment for a 'steamboat' is inexpensive and everything you will need will be available in a good Chinese supermarket, including an inexpensive 'wheel' of dishes or a Lazy Susan as we call that revolving tray with its set of fluted dishes.

Each guest will need one mesh scoop, a pair of chopsticks, chopstick 'rests', a drip tray, a rice bowl, individual sauce bowls, a cup for China tea and/or saké and a napkin.

Sesame vinegar dip

3 fl oz (85 ml) light soy sauce

2 tbsp white malt or white wine vinegar

2 tbsp white sesame seeds

1 tsp sugar

In a bowl, combine the soy sauce and vinegar. In a dry frying pan, toss and toast the sesame seeds until golden-brown, taking care not to burn them at the edges. In a blender make these into a paste with the sugar. Mix with the sauce. Serve each guest with his own little 'dipping pot'.

Fresh chilli dip

2 medium-sized green/red chillis

2 tbsp white malt or wine vinegar

2 tbsp light soy sauce

1 tsp caster sugar

Finely shred the chillis into little rings. Combine with remaining ingredients. Leave for an hour or more for the 'heat' to develop. Serve as above.

A third dip can be any of the commercial-brand black or yellow bean sauces or dips. (Watch you don't pick up a jar of bean paste.)

Won ton (Chinese dumplings)

8 oz (225 g) Won ton or Won ton 'skins'

10 oz (275 g) minced lean pork

1 tbsp light soy sauce

1 tsp salt and white or black pepper

1 tsp monosodium glutamate (optional)

1 tbsp sesame seed oil

½ small leek (white and some green), trimmed, washed and finely chopped

scant level tbsp root ginger, peeled and grated

4 fl oz (110 ml) cold water

Mix all the ingredients well together. Arrange 24 of the Won Ton skins or circles of dough on a clean work surface. Divide the filling mixture between these. Gather up the edges, twist carefully and press together. Pack in one layer covered with plastic film for transporting.

These take 5–6 minutes to cook in the steamboat. In order not to forget how long they've had or to avoid confusing cooked with part-cooked, put in the appropriate number for each guest each time. Spare 'skins' can be frozen.

Meat, seafood and vegetables (to be cooked in the 'steamboat')

- **1 packet pea noodles (transparent)**
- **12 oz (350 g) slivers pork fillet**
- **12 oz (350 g) slivers chicken breast**
- **12 large prawns, uncooked, shelled and de-veined**
- **rings of squid**
- **12 oz (350 g) slivers beef fillet**
- **24 bite-sized broccoli spears**
- **24 large washed spinach leaves**
- **24 pieces asparagus, washed and split in half**

Special chicken stock

- **bones, skin, leg meat and carcass of 3–4 lb (1.4–1.8 kg) chicken (reserve raw breasts for cooking in steamboat)**
- **1 chicken stock cube for added strength**
- **2 leeks, roughly chopped, well washed and rinsed**
- **4 fl oz (110 ml) rice wine or dry sherry**
- **1 × 2 in (5 cm) piece root ginger, peeled and sliced**
- **1 clove garlic, crushed**
- **20 white peppercorns**

Put all the chicken except the skinned breasts into a large 8–10 pt (4.5–5.5 l) pan. Well cover with 6–8 pt (3.5–4.5 l) cold water and bring to the boil slowly. Simmer for 5–10 minutes. Skim off the scum which will have risen to the surface. Add all the remaining ingredients. (*Note* No salt or herbs). Bring to the boil again, and cook at a very gentle rolling boil *un*lidded, for 1¼–1½ hours. Allow to cool. Decant off the clear stock through a sieve lined with a muslin or clean cloth. Cool. Refrigerate. Transport in 2 screw-top plastic flagons. The second one is for topping up.

A SCANDINAVIAN PICNIC

In 1967 Glyndebourne travelled to Scandinavia taking productions of Cimarosa's 'Il Matrimonio Segreto' and Mozart's 'Don Giovanni'. Each a very apt production for the smaller-scale houses in Oslo, Stockholm and Copenhagen, and particularly for the charming eighteenth-century theatre of the Royal Palace at Drottningholm in Sweden.

My first venture abroad, after my initial training as an hôtelier at Lausanne's hotel school, was to Copenhagen, where I worked for two years as a student at The Palace Hotel in Raadhuspladsen. Whilst there I was released to gain some few months' experience at Stockholm's Grand Hotel. It was in Copenhagen's Kongensnytov (King's New Square) that I saw my first opera in a foreign country – Smetana's 'The Bartered Bride' – performed in the rather uncomfortable Konigs' Teater.

At the time, after the drab years of the Second World War in Britain, it was an eye-opener to see food prepared as simply, and served as freely, as it was in Sweden and Denmark. I encountered not only Sweden's elaborate cold table, but also, and not to be confused with it, the ubiquitous *smørrebrød*, or open sandwich, in Denmark.

All Danes eat open sandwiches daily: if not at lunchtime, then in the evening. The *madpak*, or sandwich box, is carried by people of all ages and all walks of life and every restaurant features a large menu of *smørrebrød* which literally means 'butter breads'. These open sandwiches and their colourful, intriguing toppings are in a class of their own for they are neither sandwiches nor salads as we know them. They do make perfect picnic fare presented, as in Denmark, on a large shallow tray and served with a flat spatula, to be eaten with a knife and fork.

Spiced Crab-Stuffed Eggs
Creamed Cod
Cheese Mousse
Chicken, Apple and Walnut Salad

Cold Pâté-Stuffed Duckling
Sweet Pickled Beetroot
Danish Cucumber Salad
Sweet Onion Salad

Rød Grød Med Fløde
(this is a cold fruit gruel or soup)
Danish Sweet Lemon Soup

The *smörgåsbord* of Sweden is a grander version of Denmark's *koldbord* or cold table. It stems from the days when the Swedes living in their sparsely scattered country

farms and homes would gather together for a family wedding or other such communal entertainment. Guests would arrive bearing their particular speciality as a supplement to the menu and to add variety to the hostess's table; not unlike the Faith Teas of war-torn Britain where sharing was the order of things. Much – though by no means all – of the *smörgåsbord* is based on fish dishes, each of which lends itself to the picnic hamper. For a Scandinavian picnic the best bread is a medium or light Danish rye. If this is not available, then opt for German Pumpernickel. Good-quality English white bread will suffice for milder toppings. Don't have too much bread – it is merely a fulcrum – it should measure 2½ × 4½ in (6 × 11 cm) at the most. The quality of the butter is also important. Use the creamy, lightly-salted Danish butter and spread it over the whole surface of the bread right up to the edges. This serves as a barrier to the marinades and sauces and therefore prevents the bread from becoming soggy.

Next in importance is the lettuce leaf. An open sandwich always has a crisp, curly, green lettuce leaf both to contain the toppings and to give the essential 'lift' to the ensemble.

The base is now ready to receive any one of an enormous variety of toppings. Below is my anglicised version of a simple but effective Scandinavian Picnic Buffet.

Spiced crab-stuffed eggs

12 eggs, hard-boiled

wholewheat bread or toast

Filling

6 oz (175 g) butter, softened

1 small freshly dressed crab (about 8–10 oz/225–275 g) weighed after dressing

2 oz (50 g) Parmesan cheese, freshly grated

1 heaped tsp Colman's tarragon mustard

2 heaped tsp Baie Roses (pink peppercorns in brine)

1 clove garlic, crushed

2 good dashes Tabasco sauce

1 tsp salt

good squeeze of lemon juice

2 heaped tsp tomato purée

1 tbsp freshly chopped tarragon (or parsley)

1 tsp milled black pepper

Cut a small piece off the top and bottom of each egg. Empty the eggs with an apple corer by gently plunging it down the centre from top to bottom. Put all the filling ingredients plus the hard-boiled egg yolks into a blender or food processor. Mix until smooth. Press through a hair sieve.

Using a large rose tube fitted into a piping bag, pipe the mixture into the eggs. Fit a 'cap' of egg white. Spread any remaining mixture on to circles of wholewheat bread or toast. Stand an egg on top of each circle. Serve at room temperature.

Serves 6

Creamed cod

Delicious for a fork luncheon on a warm spring or summer's day. It looks marvellous as a finished dish.

3 lb (1.4 kg) cod fillet, skinned

Court bouillon

1 onion, sliced

½ pt (275 ml) dry white wine

juice and zest of 1 lemon

salt

8–10 peppercorns

Dressing

½ pt (275 ml) soured cream

½ pt (275 ml) single cream

12 oz (350 g) cottage cheese

salt and milled white pepper

juice of ½ lemon

1–2 dashes of Tabasco

cold, strained cooking liquor

Garnish

1 cucumber, peeled, halved, seeded and cut into ¼ in (6 mm) segments

4 hard-boiled eggs, segmented

freshly chopped dill, parsley, chives or any fresh green herbs

shrimps or prawns

Bring the ingredients for the *court bouillon* to the boil with 1 pt (575 ml) water and simmer for 10 minutes. Cut the cod into pieces, add to the *court bouillon*, simmer for 5 minutes, covered. Leave to cool in the liquor for 30 minutes. Drain, retaining the liquor. Remove any bones. Flake coarsely with your fingers. Cool completely. Chill, covered with plastic film.

Using a metal spoon, fold first the soured cream then the single cream into the cheese. Season well with salt, milled white pepper, lemon juice and the odd dash of Tabasco. If necessary, add a little of the cold liquor to arrive at a loose but not runny consistency. Carefully fold in the chilled flaked fish. Pile the mixture into a china or glass serving dish and garnish using the ingredients listed above, or as desired.

If the dish has to wait a while before being served, cover lightly with a plastic film or a clean napkin wrung out in cold water, and store in the refrigerator. *Serves 6–8*

Cheese mousse

½ pt (275 ml) chicken stock

2 sachets gelatine crystals

1½ lb (700 g) cottage cheese

1 tsp black pepper

1 heaped tsp paprika

1 tsp salt

juice of ½ lemon

½ pt (275 ml) double cream, whipped to soft peak

2 egg whites, stiffly beaten

Bring the chicken stock to the boil. Turn off the heat. Sprinkle in the gelatine crystals and stir until dissolved. Leave to cool but not set. In a blender or food processor, blend the cheese with all the seasoning, cooled chicken stock and lemon juice. Transfer to a large bowl. Incorporate the whipped cream thoroughly. Cut and fold in the stiffly beaten egg whites. Pour the mousse into a ring mould or glass bowl. Put to set overnight.

Chicken, apple and walnut salad

3–4 lb (1.4–1.8 kg) chicken

½ pt (275 ml) French dressing

3 red-skinned apples

juice of 1 lemon

6 oz (175 g) walnut halves, roughly crushed

¾ pt (425 ml) mayonnaise (home-made or bought)

Stock

2 carrots, cleaned and cut into pieces

6 sticks celery

2 onions, peeled

1 sachet bouquet garni

salt as necessary

Garnish

2 oz (50 g) walnut halves

freshly chopped parsley and watercress

First cook the bird, either early in the day or the previous day. Try to avoid over-refrigerating it once cooked as this does tend to dry out the meat. Unless the weather is exceptionally hot, it can be left covered in a cool larder, overnight.

Put the bird in a pan with the stock ingredients and enough cold water to cover (about 2 pt (1.1 l). Bring to the boil, take off any scum and simmer for about 1–1½ hours. Leave to cool, then skin, bone and cut the meat into bite-sized pieces. Splash with French dressing before it is completely cold.

Quarter and core the apples but do not peel them. Cut into small pieces. Toss in lemon juice to prevent discolouring. Mix with the chicken and crushed walnuts. Bind the chicken, apple and nut mixture with the mayonnaise. If home-made mayonnaise is too stiff, whisk in a spoon or two of cold stock before adding to chicken. Pile the mixture into a serving dish and garnish.
Serves 6

Cold pâté-stuffed duckling

1 cold roast duck or duckling

Filling

1 × 12 oz (350 g) tin Swiss Parfait

6 oz (175 g) unsalted butter

1 tsp nutmeg

1 tsp black pepper

squeeze of lemon juice

3 tbsp whisky or rum

Cut the breasts off the duck by cutting down either side of the breast bone, following the wish-bone round. Carefully lift each breast away, cutting where it adheres to the carcass. Lay the breasts side by side on a cutting board and, holding the knife at an angle of 45 degrees, cut diagonal pieces ½ in (1.2 cm) thick. You should get 7–8 slices from each side.

Make a fine purée of the pâté ingredients and rub this through a sieve. Fill a piping bag fitted with a rose tube with half the mixture. Spread the remaining pâté on the bared breast and lay it back where it came from! Finally, pipe a column of rich pâté down the centre of the breasts, using any left over as you please.
Serves 8 as a first course or use as part of a buffet

Sweet pickled beetroot

It is so simple to prepare pickled beetroot at home that it seems a shame to spend money on buying it. It keeps for 2–3 weeks in the refrigerator.

1 lb (450 g) beetroot

½ pt (275 ml) wine vinegar

¼ pt (150 ml) water

2 oz (50 g) sugar

few strips of fresh horseradish

Wash the beetroots but do not peel them. Cook them in water until tender, about 1½–2 hours. Allow to cool, then peel and slice them. Pack the slices into screw-top glass jars. Bring vinegar, water, sugar and horseradish to the boil and pour over the beets until they are completely covered. The beetroot should taste slightly sweet and sour. Cover the jars for storage.
Makes 1 lb (450 g)

Sweet onion salad

1 lb (450 g) tiny pickling onions

4 fl oz (110 ml) red wine vinegar

4 fl oz (110 ml) olive oil

3 oz (75 g) tomato purée

2 bay leaves

½ tsp dried thyme

parsley stalks (optional)

6 oz (175 g) seedless raisins or sultanas

1 oz (25 g) brown sugar

salt

freshly milled pepper

fresh basil (optional garnish)

Peel the onions and put in a pan with all the remaining ingredients and 6 fl oz (170 ml) water. Cover, bring to the boil and simmer for 15–20 minutes, until the onions are tender but not collapsed. If the sauce is not thick enough remove the onions with a draining spoon and boil the sauce rapidly until it is viscous. Cool, chill in the refrigerator.

Serve in individual ramekins or glasses with a small wedge of lemon and French bread and butter. If, in the summer months, you have some fresh basil, use a little chopped and sprinkled over the onions.

Serves 6

Danish cucumber salad

1 good cucumber

2 tsp salt

Dressing

3 tbsp white wine vinegar

1 tbsp water

1 tbsp lemon juice

2 oz (50 g) caster sugar

1 tsp milled white pepper

Mix all the ingredients for the dressing well together. Wash the cucumber, dry it and slice it thinly on a food processor or mandoline. Put the sliced cucumber into a bowl and sprinkle with the salt mixing well in with the hand or a slotted spoon.

Cover with a plate and weight this down to press out the juices. Leave for an hour or so. Squeeze or press out all the bitter juices and discard. Put the cucumber into a clean bowl and mix with the dressing.

Serves 4–6 as part of a buffet

Rød grød med fløde

This delicious Danish red fruit purée can also be made with gooseberries, putting in a couple of elderberry flower heads to give a subtle scent, and adding a drop or two of green colouring.

2 lb (900 g) red berries (any combination of raspberries, blackberries, red- or black-currants, cherries and strawberries)

6 oz (175 g) caster sugar

2 tbsp lemon juice

2 heaped tsp potato flour

red food colouring

caster sugar

In a stainless steel or enamel pan gradually bring to the boil the fruit, sugar, lemon juice and a little water. Simmer until completely fallen. Strain. Make the syrup up to ¾ pt (425 ml) with water. Bring back to the boil.

Slake the potato flour into a teacup of cold water. As the syrup is boiling, stir in the mixture a little at a time, allowing the potato flour to thicken the syrup between each addition. Add only enough red colour to make the syrup bright. Stop stirring in the potato flour as soon as the mixture is thick enough. Stir in the strained fruit. Dredge the surface with caster sugar to stop a skin from forming. Cool, then chill.

Note Potato flour is essential here, as it thickens without clouding.

Serves 6

Danish sweet lemon soup

Sweet soups *are* good and are easy to prepare – do give them a try. They are particularly nice at a garden lunch after a light main course. This one is very delicious and nourishing: my children when youngsters used to like it served as they do in Denmark, with raw porridge oats sprinkled on top.

2 oz (50 g) caster sugar

4 egg yolks

finely grated rind and juice of 3 lemons

1 pt (575 ml) buttermilk

Whisk the sugar and yolks until white, then add the juice and rind of the lemons, and finally stir in the buttermilk. Chill well. Transport in a thermos flask with ice cubes and extra lemon slices.

Serves 4

THE ITALIAN PICNIC

Italy and opera are inextricably intertwined (opera, after all, was born in Italy) and this connection is mirrored in the special relationship between Glyndebourne and Italy. True, I can think of no olive trees or pungent-smelling Roman pines in the Glyndebourne gardens, but, despite the quintessentially English setting of the South Downs, the atmosphere of Italy is always alive through the summer. There is usually at least one Italian-language opera in the repertoire bringing with it visiting Italian singers who will quickly make themselves at home, seek out the delicatessen that sells the most authentic Italian groceries and hospitably set out to prove that Italian food, when properly cooked, can taste really Italian even in Sussex.

The king of the Italian culinary feast at Glyndebourne was the bass-baritone, Renato Capecchi. He would greet you at the door of his small flat in Brighton in a chef's hat (he is already over 6 foot tall) and proceed to deliver like a proud midwife course after course of exquisite food (antipasto, home-made brodo, three kinds of pasta, two kinds of fish, veal, three vegetables, etc, etc). The very flicker of an incipient refusal of any one of these intricately prepared dishes would send Renato into utmost despair.

The picnic below is a much more modest affair, but is beautiful to look at and sunny in character. It is quite filling and you may decide to serve fruit instead of the Torrone Molle, although the latter could be left until after the performance and eaten accompanied by a small glass of *grappa* (that wonderful if rather dangerous Italian *eau de vie*) in celebration of an exquisite evening of Italian music and food. If you serve fruit, choose large soft purple figs, ripe and juicy nectarines or peaches, eaten with the help of huge table napkins to catch the drips. If you decide to offer cheese, try some Taleggio, or a fresh hunk of Parmesan to nibble in the fingers. As with all Italian and Mediterranean cookery, the authenticity of taste depends much on the quality of olive oil used. It must be real extra-virgin, dense, dark greeny-gold oil.

Cold Pasta Salad with Squid and Prawns

Pollo Tonnato
Cold Spinach Salad
Tomato and Basil Salad

Torrone Molle
Fresh Fruit
Cheese (Taleggio or Parmesan)

Cold pasta salad with squid and prawns

8 oz (225 g) fresh squid

1 glass dry white wine

6 oz (175 g) frozen prawns

3 tbsp best virgin olive oil

1 medium onion, finely chopped

1 large, 2 small cloves garlic

8 oz (225 g) fresh ripe tomatoes

1 lemon

salt

black pepper, freshly ground

12 oz (350g) pasta (rigatoni, shells or bows)

8 Italian black olives, halved and stoned

2 tbsp chopped parsley (preferably Italian)

If you have bought fresh squid from the fishmonger, clean it carefully in cold water, removing the hard bony bits, rinse well, and slice into rings. If you got them ready cleaned, just rinse and slice them. Put them in a small saucepan with the wine and stew gently until tender (about 20 minutes). Put the prawns on a plate to defrost. Heat the oil in a heavy-bottomed pan, add the onion and fry gently until transparent but not brown, then add the crushed garlic and cook again for a few minutes. Peel and chop the tomatoes and add to the onions turning the flame up to cook fiercely for a few minutes, or until the liquid begins to evaporate. This should not take more than 4 minutes as you want the tomatoes tasting fresh, not stewed. Add the squid (without the wine), the prawns (without the defrozen juice) and the finely grated rind of the lemon. Add salt and pepper to taste and turn off the heat.

In the meantime cook the pasta in plenty of boiling salted water until *al dente*, drain well and mix with 1 tbsp of olive oil to avoid sticking. Add the tomato and squid mixture, the olives and the parsley and mix gently but thoroughly, adding a little more oil if you think it needs it.

Put the pasta in a generous earthenware dish, cover with foil or Clingfilm and put in the fridge until ready to pack for the picnic. This dish does not need to be kept very cold so you can transport it in a basket or direct in the car.

Pollo tonnato

1 medium sized roasting chicken

1 tbsp oil

salt and black pepper, freshly ground

1 small onion

1 small carrot

1 stick celery

1 small glass white wine

1 tin tuna fish

½ pt (275 ml) mayonnaise

capers

1 tin anchovies

Rub the chicken with the oil and salt and pepper and lightly brown it in a heavy pot. Add the chopped vegetables and the white wine and pot-roast it for 1¼ hours. Remove from the oven and strain the juices into a basin. When they are cool, skim the fat off the top and melt down to a cold running consistency.

Open the tin of tuna and strain off the oil then put it in a food processor or liquidizer with ¼ pt (150 ml) of the stock. Process until smooth, adding more of the stock if it is too stiff. It is important that the stock should not be hot because it will curdle the mayonnaise when you add it; the mixture at this stage should be the consistency of lightly whipped cream. Pour the mayonnaise into a bowl and add the tuna mixture until the right flavour is reached – some people like the sauce more mayonnaisey, some more fishy. Add salt and pepper to taste.

Carefully take the flesh off the chicken and place the meat, in fairly large chunks, on a flat dish. Pour the sauce over, decorate with the capers and anchovies and cool in the fridge until ready to pack for the picnic. The sauce will stiffen slightly when it has cooled. This dish is not suitable to take on a hot day unless you have a cool-box because any mayonnaise-based sauce is likely to separate if kept warm for too long.

Cold spinach salad

2 lb (900 g) fresh young spinach

sea salt, freshly ground

¼ pt (150 ml) best virgin olive oil

juice of 1 lemon

black pepper, freshly ground

Wash the spinach well and put it, with no more water other than that already clinging to it, in a large pan with some salt. Boil fiercely until tender and still bright green (about 3 minutes) then drain very well having first refreshed it under running cold water. Press the spinach down on the sieve with the back of a wooden spoon to get all the water out.

Put it in a white china dish and add the oil, lemon juice, salt and pepper and mix with a fork. Taste for seasoning and add more as necessary. Cover and put it in the fridge until ready to pack for the picnic. This dish can be transported in a cool-box or an ordinary basket – it is very untemperamental and a little goes a long way.

Tomato and basil salad

12 oz (350 g) fresh, ripe tomatoes – preferably of the Continental type. Don't be tempted to buy the hard rather limey green ones piled up in supermarkets – they taste of absolutely nothing, even if you leave them a couple of days to ripen.

2 tbsp best virgin oil

sea salt, freshly ground

black pepper, freshly ground

a few drops of Balsamic vinegar if you have it (acceto Balsamico is a dark brown, mild and slightly sweet vinegar, available from the very best delicatessens)

2–3 sprigs of lush, large-leaved basil

Don't be tempted to peel the tomatoes as they will go to watery mush during the journey. Slice them and put them in a white china dish. Add a tablespoon or two of best-quality olive oil, the salt, pepper and Balsamic vinegar. Tear the basil into small pieces or cut it with kitchen scissors rather than chop it – the juices in the fresh green leaves will be left behind on your chopping board if you do. Mix the salad carefully. Take some whole leaves separately in a plastic bag to put on at the last minute. Cover and refrigerate before packing in your picnic box or basket.

Torrone Molle

This luscious confection is a chocoholic's dream, though made in this recipe with cocoa rather than real chocolate. I find the dense bitterness of the cocoa contrasts better with the biscuits and accompanying cream.

4 oz (110 g) butter

4 oz (110 g) ground almonds

4 oz (110 g) cocoa

4 oz (110 g) caster sugar

1 large egg

4 oz (110 g) *petit beurre* biscuits (or Osborne)

whipped cream or Jersey cream

Soften the butter and mix it together with the ground almonds and cocoa in a food processor. Melt the sugar with a little water over a low heat until the sugar is melted and add it to the mixture in the processor. Beat the egg and add it too. Break the biscuits very gently into pieces the size of 1 p pieces, being careful not to crumble them too much. Place the chocolate mixture in a mixing bowl, add the biscuits and mix together with extreme care so the biscuits don't turn into crumbs. Line a loaf tin with oiled tin-foil and pack the mixture into it pushing it down into the corners. Cover and refrigerate for several hours, and overnight if possible.

Transport in a cool-box, preferably in the tin it is made in, and also take a long flat plate to turn it out onto. Alternatively, you can turn it out at home and wrap it in at least two layers of fresh tin-foil, then put it on top in the cool box so it does not crush.

You will need cream with it – either lightly whipped cream taken in a bowl or a carton of Jersey cream.

A MEDITERRANEAN PICNIC

All Mediterranean countries have some indefinable quality in common – an almost tangible atmosphere for which so many people in more northern countries yearn. Look at the number of operas which have common origins around the Mediterranean sea: 'Carmen', 'The Barber' and 'Don Giovanni', all leading very different lives in Seville; Greeks on Crete, Ariadne on Naxos, Turks in Italy, Italians in Turkey . . . the list goes on. What is it that brings them together? Is it just the sun, the olive groves, the evening light on rose-coloured hills? Or the 'wine dark' sea itself, fickle, unpredictable and tantalizing? Whatever it is, the Mediterranean has an allure to composers as diverse as Mozart and Rossini, Purcell and Strauss, as it always has had to poets, painters and sculptors from all over the world. And to cooks too.

For cooks the attraction is the drama and vividness of the natural ingredients: brilliantly coloured vegetables, sparkling silver fish, intense shiny black olives – nothing gentle and mellifluous as you might find in a Sussex country garden. And yet despite certain common factors, for instance the use of olive oil rather than butter for most cooking, the plentiful use of tomatoes, onions and garlic, and fish and seafood, each country bordering on the Mediterranean has a distinct style of its own, and so do the various regions of each country. In this picnic I have chosen dishes which work well together even though they may come from different countries. They will all 'travel' well, none needing to be kept very cold and will look their best served off rough earthenware dishes.

As the garlic wafts gently over the hedge to your next door neighbour's rather conservative picnic of smoked salmon, brown bread and butter and strawberries, you will be delighted you decided to be more adventurous.

Taramasalata and
Aubergine Purée with
Olive and Fresh Thyme Bread

Pissaladière
Lentil Salad
Courgette Salad with Pine Nuts and Raisins
Mediterranean Salad

Greek Honey Cheesecake with
Apricot Purée Sauce

Taramasalata

A Mediterranean *hors d'oeuvre* is normally a very simple affair consisting of olives, salamis, salads of pimentos or tomatoes, perhaps some fish or prawns. In Greece you will find in addition taramasalata, humous, and tahina paste. Of course all these delicacies, once only found in specialist shops in Soho or known to the seasoned traveller, are now readily available in large supermarkets and bought alongside marmite and corn flakes in the weekly shop for the children's tea. No-one, of course, really thinks that the bright pink concoction called taramasalata that you buy on the deli–counter bears any resemblance to the pale flesh-coloured paste you eat with a glass of Ouzo while dabbling your toes in the Mediterranean, but many may prefer it and most will know no difference.

My suggestion for an *hors d'oeuvre* for this Mediterranean picnic is to take the time and trouble to make one or two of these classic goodies rather than buy them ready-made. You will be astonished and pleased with the difference and so will your guests.

Genuine tarama is the dried eggs of grey mullet, but that will be impossible to find in England, so we have to make do with smoked cod's roe.

8 oz (225 g) smoked cod's roe, previously soaked in water for a couple of hours

juice of ½ lemon

½ pt (275 ml) mild olive oil

boiling water

1 or 2 cloves garlic

black pepper

Remove the skin from the cod's roe and put it in a blender with the lemon juice. Blend until smooth then, with the machine still on, add the oil drop by drop as if you were making mayonnaise. It will become very thick so you will need to add a little boiling water to keep the consistency smooth and fairly soft. Continue until all the oil has been used up then add the crushed garlic and black pepper to taste. If you find the finished paste too heavy you can lighten it by adding a piece of white bread with the crusts removed which you have previously soaked in cold water and squeezed out. Add it to the cod's roe at the start and proceed as above. It will make the taste milder and the consistency less sticky.

Aubergine purée

This is another hors d'oeuvre with a marvellous smoky flavour, to eat with bread or toast, and is made in a very similar manner to taramasalata.

3 large aubergines

2 cloves garlic

salt

pepper

¼ pt (150 ml) olive oil

juice of ½ lemon

chopped parsley

Grill the aubergines, turning them over and over to blacken their skins. When soft, skin them and purée in a food processor together with the garlic, salt and pepper. Then add the olive oil drop by drop as for mayonnaise. Lastly add the lemon juice and parsley.

Both these dishes should be served with fresh crusty bread. In some specialist Greek shops you can get marvellous olive bread or herb bread, and either would be perfect – or make your own. Put the taramasalata and the aubergine purée in separate chunky earthenware dishes and serve a separate dish of olives with them. What sort of olives? Small nutty black ones, large luminous purple ones, sleek oblong green ones? Lawrence Durrell described the taste of black olives as 'a taste older than meat, older than wine. A taste as old as cold water.' For a special meal like this it is worth going to the shop with the best selection you know of, then taste, discuss, taste again and finally buy.

Olive and fresh thyme bread

½ oz (15 g) dried yeast
1 tsp soft brown sugar
6 tbsp warm water
8 oz (225 g) wholemeal flour
8 oz (225 g) white bread flour
1 tsp salt
1 oz (25 g) lard, or other hard cooking fat
3 oz (75 g) black olives, stoned and cut into pieces
1 tsp chopped fresh thyme or dried thyme
just under ½ pt (275 ml) mixed water and milk

Sprinkle the dried yeast and brown sugar onto the water, stir briefly and leave to activate in a warm place. Meanwhile sift the flours and salt into a large basin and rub in the fat. Add the chopped olives and the thyme. Pour in the yeast mixture and the water and milk and mix to a soft dough using more or less of the liquid as necessary. Pull about and knead for at least 5 minutes then put into a greased and floured loaf tin (or shape into rounds on a greased baking sheet). Allow to rise in a warmish place until the bread rises above the top of the tin (or the rounds have nearly doubled in size).

Bake towards the top of a hot oven (450°F/230°C/Reg 8) for 15 minutes. Reduce the heat to 400°F(200°C)Reg 6 and bake for a further 20–25 minutes for loaves, 15–20 for rounds. Cool on a rack and wrap in a fresh tea towel to take to the picnic.

Pissaladière

The true pissaladière, which is the southern French equivalent of the pizza, has a base of bread dough and a filling of slowly stewed onions, anchovies and olives. By the addition of tomatoes (which is quite authentic) and by replacing the bread dough with a pastry case the dish immediately becomes lighter and a touch more elegant whilst retaining its earthy origins and wonderful aromatic flavours of the Mediterranean.

Pastry case

4 oz (110 g) butter and lard, mixed
8 oz (225 g) flour
water

Rub the fat into the flour, add enough water to make a firm dough. Roll into a ball, cover and refrigerate for 30 minutes. Roll out the pastry to 11 in (28 cm) diameter and fill a 10 in (25 cm) flan ring. Leave to rest, then bake blind (by putting paper and dried beans in the pastry to keep its shape) for 10 minutes in a hot oven (425°F/220°C/Reg 7). Remove the paper and bake a further 5–10 minutes until the pastry is light golden brown and crisp.

Filling

good virgin olive oil
1½ lb (700 g) large onions, chopped
3 cloves of garlic
1 lb (450 g) ripe fleshy tomatoes
1 tbsp tomato paste
2 tbsp fresh basil (or parsley if unavailable)
1 tsp fresh chopped thyme or oregano
salt and freshly ground black pepper
2 tbsp dry breadcrumbs
12 flat anchovy fillets
12 black olives
1 tbsp fresh parsley

Melt the olive oil in a large heavy-bottomed frying pan and add the onions and the garlic. Cover and sauté very slowly, stirring occasionally for 15–20 minutes or until a soft, transparent pale golden colour. They must not brown so keep watching them. Skin the tomatoes, remove the seeds and hard core and chop coarsely. Turn up the heat and add the tomatoes to the onion mixture, cooking fairly fiercely until all the moisture has evaporated. Turn the heat down again and add the tomato paste, basil, thyme and salt and pepper to taste.

Sprinkle the pastry shell with the breadcrumbs to absorb any excess moisture and spoon the tomato-onion mixture into it, smoothing the top with the back of a spoon. Lay the anchovies criss-cross on the filling, with the stoned black olives dotted between them. Put in a moderate oven for 20 minutes. Remove, cool and sprinkle with parsley.

It is advisable to keep the tart in its tin when transporting it to the picnic, only removing the outside when you are ready to serve it.

Lentil salad

This recipe is very far removed from the steaming stodgy mass of orange lentil stew found in Northern Europe. It is much more similar in taste and texture to the North African couscous salads, now found in sad tasteless imitations in supermarket deli-counters. It is essential to use the right lentils; they must be either the large brown variety, or the little French slatey-green coloured ones which end up brown when cooked. Use red or yellow ones and they will turn into a mush. Neither the brown nor green lentils need to be soaked.

12 oz (350 g) lentils
salt and black pepper
bouquet garni of thyme, parsley and bay leaf
6 cloves garlic
1 large or 2 small carrots
1 onion
1 stick celery
8 tbsp best virgin olive oil
1 tbsp red wine vinegar
2 tbsp chopped parsley

Rinse the lentils and put them in a pan with enough water to cover them barely, add 1 tsp salt, the bouquet garni and 3 cloves of garlic wrapped in a piece of cheesecloth and bring to the boil. Simmer gently for 10 minutes stirring occasionally. Finely dice the carrot, onion and celery and add to the lentils. Simmer for a further 10–15 minutes until the lentils are *al dente* but cooked. If necessary, add a little more water to prevent them from sticking but there should be very little water left when the lentils are done. Toss them immediately in 4 tbsp olive oil and spread them out on baking sheets to cool to room temperature, discarding the bouquet garni.

In the bowl in which you are going to serve the salad pour the rest of the olive oil, the vinegar, the rest of the garlic, minced, and the parsley. Put in the lentils and carefully but thoroughly mix them together, adding more salt and freshly ground black pepper to taste.

Alice Waters, the inspired and inspiring American cook, adds goat's cheese to this salad, which makes it much more substantial – perhaps more suitable for a starter with small ripe tomatoes. It is, however, exquisite, and you may like to crumble in a little bit of goat's cheese with the dressing for this salad.

Courgette salad with pine nuts and raisins

1 lb (450 g) courgettes, no larger than ¾ in (2 cm) diameter
2 tbsp best virgin olive oil
2 cloves garlic, crushed
1 tbsp pine nuts
1 tbsp raisins
salt and pepper
lemon juice

Slice the courgettes in ¼ in (6 mm) rounds and throw into fiercely boiling salted water for 1 minute. Drain well, patting them dry with kitchen paper.

Heat the olive oil in a frying pan and add the garlic and the pine nuts. Sauté gently until the nuts are coloured then add the courgettes, turning them over until lightly sautéed but still *al dente*. Take off the heat, add the raisins, salt, pepper and lemon juice to taste. Mix well and put in a white china dish. This dish can be made with slivered almonds instead of pine nuts.

Mediterranean salad

It is important to have something crisp and fresh to go alongside the oil-based recipes in this chapter, so here is a simple Mediterranean salad.

1 crisp lettuce of the Webb's variety

1 head radicchio

½ sweet Spanish onion

1 orange

Take the outer leaves off the lettuce, wash it, dry it and break it up in a salad bowl. Cut the hard core out of the radicchio, take the leaves off and add them to the lettuce. Finely slice the onion (as much as you wish) and add it to the lettuces. Finally peel the orange – dunk it in boiling water for 1 minute before peeling as this helps you to remove all the pith. Cut it up on a plate and add it, juice and all, to the lettuce. Mix well, cover and pack for the picnic. Take salt and pepper separately.

Greek honey cheesecake with apricot purée

Ices, yoghurts and fresh fruit are the main constituents of the Mediterranean pudding diet. The Spanish go in for Crème Caramel-type sweets, the Arabs and Greeks prefer sweeter, heavier cakes made with almonds, honey, eggs and sugar.

Some of these are rather too much for northern tastes and this cheesecake is lighter and delicious.

6 digestive biscuits

1 oz (25 g) butter

8 oz (225 g) curd cheese

2 oz (50 g) runny honey

2 oz (50 g) caster sugar

1 whole egg

1 extra white of egg

Crush the digestive biscuits into crumbs. Melt the butter and pour it into a slightly warmed 8 in (20 cm) white china flan dish with fairly deep sides (at least 1 in/2.5 cm). Make sure the butter covers the sides and bottom of the dish. Pour in the crumbs and pat them all over until they too cover the bottom and sides.

Soften the cheese with a fork. Warm the honey and pour it in with the cheese, add the sugar and the egg yolk and beat thoroughly until smooth. Whisk the 2 egg whites until they hold soft peaks and fold them into the cheese mixture. Pour into the dish and bake in the centre of a moderate oven until cooked (about 25–30 minutes). Leave to cool and sprinkle a little powdered cinnamon on the top.

Apricot purée sauce

1 lb (450 g) fresh or 12 oz (350 g) dried apricots which have been soaked for 8 hours

1 small wine glass of sweet white wine

soft brown sugar to taste (quantities depend on the ripeness of the fresh apricots and the quality of the dried ones)

Stew the apricots in the wine and some sugar until cooked. Strain, retaining the juices, and put them through a mouli or sieve adding enough juice to arrive at a thick though fluid pouring consistency. Check for sweetness, adding more sugar if necessary. Put in a jar with a screw top or a plastic pot with well-fitting lid to take to the picnic.

At home I would finish this pudding off with lightly roasted slivered almonds (served hot) but this is unpracticable for the picnic. You could take some cold roasted almonds separately if you wished, and cream.

THE HARVEST HAMPER

To me the honeyed scent of melons, the hue of russet apples, the sight of tense-skinned aubergines and tomatoes, the deep green coats of crisp, cold cucumbers – this is what fruit and vegetables are all about.

Evocative paragraphs on visits to ancient market places in Provence, bordered by swaying oleanders and garlands of mimosa, are only too stimulating and the very thought of a pannier of cool and cooling *crudités* with an attendant pool of *aioli*, of rich red and yellow *pepperoni*, of bowls of blushing peaches and luscious nectarines are impossibly mouthwatering, but these are words for other shores – for Provence, for the Tuscan hills of Italy or for the white beaches of some remote Greek island. They spell out heat and heady, lavender-scented airs and it would be unfair to evoke such an atmosphere for a picnic that is vegetarian (though my pen stalls in my hand when I come to write such an uninviting word), planned for the sylvan setting of the now-legendary Sussex hayfield.

A garden feast sounds more promising. The label vegetarian instantly suggests stereotyped dishes dubbed 'wholesome' or 'crunchy', which almost all seem to demand yoghurt as an ingredient, are certainly nut-laden in a rather solid way and are served with cumbersome salads.

None of this inspires the mind nor is it right for a picnic at Glyndebourne. Elegant, light-textured, with eye appeal is nearer the mark and ought not to be beyond our scope. Consider, too, the question of your fellow guests. They should be of a similar mind to yours – for the average man feels cheated, if not embarrassed , when confronted with a menu that he feels has no apparent core in the form of meat, fish or poultry.

So let me give you a menu with a shape and style which will please if not enchant the conformist; where the first Italian-inspired course is recognizable as such; where the main

Cold Green Linguine with a Strawberry and Red Pepper Cream Sauce

---

Savoury Pecan Roulade with Asparagus Tips
Cold Risotto with Saffron
Baked Aubergine and Tomato Mould

Peppered Pears in Red Wine

course is unusual, light-textured but filling enough to satisfy and in which there is an elegant dessert, making an ideal end to a balmy interlude.

Cold green linguine with a strawberry and red pepper cream sauce

Sauce

2 large ripe red peppers
2 tbsp olive or soy oil
2 shallots *or* 1 oz (25 g) onion, finely chopped
1 large clove garlic, crushed
½ vegetable stock cube
1 heaped tsp sweet paprika
¼ tsp mild curry powder
2 tsp caster sugar
1 tsp salt and pepper
6 large ripe strawberries, quartered
¼ pt (150 ml) single cream (optional)

Garnish

1 small red pepper, seeded, cut into very fine julienne strips
8oz (225 g) strawberries, sliced

Pasta

1½ lb (700 g) green linguine or other 'strand' pasta
salted water
2 tbsp olive or soy oil

To make the sauce, skin the peppers by spearing each one on a long-tined fork and fully blistering over a flame (takes 5–10 minutes). Or brush the peppers with oil, preheat the oven to maximum, stand the peppers on an oven tray and roast until blistered. Peel off the skin under cold running water. Cut the peppers in half, de-seed and cut away any ribs of pith. Chop roughly and put aside.

Heat the oil in a heavy-bottomed pan. Add the shallots and garlic and fry until lightly golden. Dissolve the stock cube in ¼ pt (150 ml) water. Add this plus the paprika, curry powder, sugar, salt, pepper and the large strawberries to the shallots. Add the prepared peppers and stir in. Lower the heat and cook gently for 15–20 minutes until soft. Purée in a blender and rub through a fine meshed sieve for extra refinement. Cool and stir in the cream if used. Chill well. Just before packing, mix into the julienne of red pepper and the sliced strawberries.

Cook the pasta in plenty of boiling salted water. Drain. Rinse under running cold water. Drain again. Put into a large strong plastic bag. Pour in 1 tbsp oil and 'work' this in with the hands to keep the pasta strands separated. Transport pasta and sauce separately.

Serves 6 as a starter

Savoury pecan roulade with asparagus tips

4 large eggs
½ tsp salt
½ tsp ground mace
black pepper, freshly ground
8 oz (225 g) pecan halves, crushed

Sauce

½ vegetable stock cube
3 tbsp red wine vinegar
juice of ½ orange
4 egg yolks
6 oz (175 g) hot melted butter
peel of 1 large orange, pared, finely chopped, blanched and drained
salt and pepper
mace

Filling and garnish

1 bundle fresh young asparagus, lightly cooked, green part only
12 quails' eggs, boiled, shelled and halved *or* 4 hard-boiled eggs, quartered
2 tbsp snipped chives
2 oz (50 g) pecan halves, shelled and roughly chopped

Butter and line a Swiss roll tin with paper, also buttered. Whisk the eggs with the salt and mace until thick. Season with pepper. Fold in 4 oz (110 g) of the crushed pecans and pour into the prepared tin, spreading the mixture evenly into the corners. Bake at 400°F (200°C) Reg 6 near the top of the oven for 6–8 minutes until firm to the touch in the centre.

Put a clean tea towel, wrung out in cold water, on to a flat surface. Cover this with a piece of greaseproof paper spread evenly with the remaining 4 oz (110 g) of crushed pecans. Invert the roulade on to the nuts and remove the base paper to allow the steam to escape. Then roll loosely.

To make the sauce, crumble the stock cube into the vinegar and orange juice in a saucepan and boil until reduced to 2 tbsp. Whisk the egg yolks and the reduced liquid in a bowl over gently boiling water until thick but not curdled. Remove from the heat and beat in the melted butter, drop by drop at first, then in a steady stream, whisking briskly all the time. Add the orange peel and season with salt, pepper and mace.

Unroll the roulade, spread with plenty of the sauce and arrange the asparagus tips, eggs and chives evenly over this. Spread over the remaining sauce. Re-roll the roulade.

The sauce can be made in advance and kept in the refrigerator overnight, where it will thicken slightly, in which case whisk back to consistency. Garnish with pecan halves.

Serves 6–8 as a main course

Note For those who prefer a less rich filling, use ½ pt (275 ml) soured cream mixed with 8 oz (225 g) cream or cottage cheese, seasoned to taste.

Cold risotto with saffron

1 oz (25 g) butter

2 tbsp olive or soy oil

1 medium onion, finely chopped

8 oz (225 g) Arborio, Carolina, or English pudding rice

up to 2½ pt (1.4 l) boiling vegetable or chicken stock (use 2 stock cubes)

2 sachets of saffron strands

salt and milled pepper

Finely chop the onion. In a wide-based pan, over a medium heat, melt the butter with the oil, stirring it around with a straight-edged wooden spatula to prevent it browning. Add the onion and soften this until it is transparent without letting it brown. Stir in the rice and fry for 1–2 minutes, stirring from time to time.

Ladle in about ½ pt (275 ml) of the hot stock, stir this well in, making sure that the rice at the sides of the pan is incorporated. Let the liquid bubble and as the rice starts to absorb this, add further ladles full. Carry on doing this, stirring the while, and bringing the rice on the edges into the centre so that the grains cook evenly. The whole operation will take up to 20 minutes or more.

When you have added all but ½ pt (275 ml) of the stock, the rice should be looking sticky and about the consistency of flowing porridge. Using a teaspoon, test it for done-ness. It is preferable to have it somewhat *al dente*, but this is a question of personal choice. So, continue cooking and adding a little stock until it is to your liking. The grains should just be separated and not too solid. Stir in the saffron. Season carefully with salt and milled pepper. Allow to cool. When cool, stir well with a fork to loosen the rice, adding a little olive oil to ensure the grains stay separated.

To prepare the saffron, put the small amount of threads into a teacup. Pour over 2 tbsp of boiling water. Stir well. Leave to infuse for 20 minutes or more. Pour the entire contents of the cup into the rice.

Baked aubergine and tomato mould

Tomato sauce

2 × 14 oz (400 g) tins Italian plum tomatoes

1 vegetable stock cube

1 clove garlic, crushed

2–3 dashes Tabasco sauce

1 good sprig fresh *or* 1 tsp dried basil or thyme

1 tsp sugar

Aubergine

4 medium but even-sized aubergines (about 5 in (12 cm) long)

salt

plenty of olive oil for frying

½ pt (275 ml) carton strained Greek yoghurt

extra basil or parsley for garnish, freshly chopped

milled pepper

Put all the ingredients for the sauce into a 3 pt (1.5 l) heavy-bottomed pan. Bring to the boil and simmer until a cohered pulp is arrived at (a scant ¾ pt (425 ml) when sieved). Press through a wire sieve. Cool. Reserve one-third for serving.

Meanwhile, wipe the aubergines and top and tail them. Cut into ¼ in (6 mm) thick discs, spread the discs on a clean surface and sprinkle lightly with salt to draw the bitter juices. Leave for 30 minutes, then rinse under cold water and pat dry with paper towels.

Heat 3–4 tbsp of olive oil in a large frying pan until lightly smoking. Brown the aubergines quickly on both sides, adding more oil as it is absorbed and when necessary. Layer the fried discs in a 2½ pt (1.4 l) ovenproof mould (or seamless cake tin), spreading each layer with some of the tomato sauce and yoghurt. Add an extra sprinkling of fresh basil or thyme if you like, and milled pepper. Go easy on the salt. Cover and bake at 375°F (190°C) Reg 5 for 35–40 minutes. Allow to cool before turning out and coating with the remaining sauce.

Serves 6–8 as an hors d'oeuvre; 4–5 as a first course or vegetable

Peppered pears in red wine

I picked up this interesting way of poaching pears from Augustin Paege's charming Box Tree restaurant in New York. Try it, it's good.

4 oz (110 g) caster sugar

zest of 1 orange

1 pt (575 ml) red Burgundy

2 in (5 cm) piece cinnamon

1 heaped tsp black peppercorns

8 pears

Select an enamel-lined or stainless-steel pan just large enough to hold the pears standing upright. Bring to the boil the sugar, zest, wine, cinnamon and peppercorns, reduce the heat and simmer carefully for 5 minutes.

Meanwhile, peel the pears and core them from the base. Leave the stalks on. Put the pears into the hot syrup and poach until tender, about 20 minutes, covered with a lid. You may have to add a little more wine as they should be covered to the base of the stalk, in which case add a little more sugar too. You will eventually arrive with a pan and quantities which 'fit'. Allow the mixture to cool before removing the pears with a slotted spoon and placing on a dish.

Strain the syrup and reduce to a thick consistency by boiling rapidly. Cool again, then spoon over the pears before chilling well, covered with plastic film. While I prefer to serve the pears as they are, you can serve them with thick, unsweetened pouring cream or with soured cream.

Serves 8.

AN AMERICAN PICNIC

So what does an American do if he wishes to have a picnic? He doesn't – he has a 'cook-out'. Or such is the popular British myth which, like most myths, is the truth with optional extras. The wild and noble scenery in the North American National Parks that we know from Disney nature films – with nostalgic and romantic names like Redfish Lake and Silver Creek – are, if truth be known, dotted all over with communal barbecues, picnic wardens, tables, benches and public conveniences. Disney's Wally the Brownbear, trudging two thousand miles with our wounded five-year-old hero in his teeth, just didn't keep his eyes open for the 'Picnic Place' signs.

But, wonderful though well-barbecued food is, it is definitely not to be considered for a Glyndebourne picnic. For one thing, by the time you had lit the coals, wooed them to life, let them go out and lit them again the bells for the final act would be ringing, no food eaten and your guests would be far from gruntled. Light the barbecue before the opera begins? Well, yes, but it would either be out by the interval or you would also have to cater for the Ringmer Fire Brigade. Then you have the problem of the smell of sizzling flesh and smoke wafting into your neighbours' strawberry mousses. No, there must be better ways to make our American friends feel at home.

Of course, there are plenty of American picnic gourmets who produce picnics with ne'er a T-bone steak in sight. Food in America, when not processed out of recognition, comes munificent and luscious with fifty-seven varieties of everything from milk to vinegar. Mounded mixed salads in wooden bowls groaning with nuts, herbs, cheese, vegetables and salamis; squashy metaphor-mixed cakes – banana, carrot, apple and coffee – and then there are the cookies – aaah, the cookies. If anything sums up the American

Blueberry Soup

Steak Tartare
Potato and Egg Salad with Dill and Mustard Mayonnaise
Salad of Cherry Tomatoes, Baby Corn and Mange-tout

Pecan and Orange Mousse Gâteau

way of life it is those huge, generous crazy-shaped biscuits full of nuts and squadgy lumps of soft chocolate. With all that country's space and variety, and all those resources, how could the inhabitants be expected to make small, precise, uniformly cut cookies?

Blueberry soup

We seem not to tolerate sweet-flavoured starters as readily as the Americans, but they do have a marvellous and unusual repertoire of fruit-based soups. This one is delicious and not too sweet.

1½ lb (700 g) blueberries (you can find them fresh in large supermarkets later in the summer or frozen all year round)

2 pt (1.1 l) water

3 cloves

1 stick cinnamon, 2 in (5 cm) long

2 tbsp soft brown sugar

2 whole oranges

lemon juice

3 tbsp Crème de Cassis (blackcurrant liqueur)

1 tbsp fruit vinegar (if possible blueberry; if you can't buy a fruit vinegar use Sherry or Cider Vinegar)

soured cream

Pick over the blueberries, discarding the stalks and any leaves. Put them in a large pan with the water, cloves, cinnamon, sugar and one of the oranges chopped, with its rind still on. Bring to the boil and simmer for about 10 minutes or until the berries are cooked. Cool and put through a mouli or sieve, forcing the pulp through with the back of a wooden spoon. Add the lemon juice, the juice of the second orange, the Crème de Cassis and the vinegar to taste. Grate the rind from half of one of the oranges and stir all together.

Chill well and put in a thermos flask which you have previously rinsed in iced water. Take a pot of soured cream separately with which to garnish each bowl.

Steak tartare

Many people are rather put off by the idea of eating raw meat, rather as they view raw fish before sampling a really well-made *seviche*. Of course, the meat in this recipe, utterly lean fine fresh beef, is very well flavoured and accompanied by lots of disguising goodies. Still, you *are* faced by a bright red mound of raw meat, so it is not a dish for the faint hearted.

Steak Tartare is an ancient nomadic Mongolian recipe but is eaten more in America now than anywhere else.

For this picnic recipe I have added more ingredients to the actual beef than usual, for ease of transport. Like Gaspacho, Steak Tartare is usually served with several garnishes in separate bowls or on your plate for you to add to your own taste. For a picnic it is easier to add them first and take just a few with you.

1 lb (450 g) completely lean fresh steak without a speck of fat

1 small onion, finely chopped

2 tbsp fresh parsley, finely chopped

2 tsp Dijon mustard

1 tbsp capers, chopped

Tabasco sauce

Worcestershire sauce

salt, freshly ground

black pepper, freshly ground

2 egg yolks

½ tsp lemon rind, grated

Garnish

1 head of lettuce

1 tin anchovies

8 black olives

1 small onion, finely sliced

1 tsp chives

Put the beef in a large bowl and add all the other ingredients. The Tabasco and Worcestershire sauces should be added to taste but should be treated with caution as you don't want to drown the taste of the beef completely. Cover and refrigerate until you pack up the picnic. You should prepare this as late as possible on the morning of the picnic, so that the meat has a chance to chill but not lose its colour and freshness.

Line a dish that is fairly flat but fits into your cool-box with small crispy lettuce leaves. Form the meat into a mound on top of the lettuce. Decorate with criss-crossed anchovies, the olives, capers and onion rings. Sprinkle with chopped chives, cover with two layers of tin foil and put at the top of the cool-box so it doesn't get too squashed.

Potato and egg salad with dill and mustard mayonnaise

A delicious creamy classic American salad which goes very well with the Steak Tartare. The dill is essential to its authenticity. It is a marvellous herb which does not seem to be affected by a journey even in hot weather, unlike mint and basil. Most large supermarkets now sell little packets of herbs not usually grown in our gardens.

12 oz (350 g) evenly sized new potatoes

just under ½ pt (275 ml) mayonnaise

3 tbsp soured cream

2 tbsp chopped dill

1 tbsp Dijon whole-grain mustard

salt and freshly ground black pepper

4 hard-boiled eggs

½ small onion

Scrape and wash the potatoes and cook them in salted water until tender (about 10 minutes). Drain and leave to cool. Make the sauce by mixing the mayonnaise, cream, 1 tbsp of the dill, mustard, salt and pepper together in a bowl. Halve the potatoes, quarter the eggs, and very finely slice the onion. Pour on the sauce and mix together very carefully so the egg doesn't disintegrate. Transfer to the bowl in which you are to serve it, sprinkle the remaining dill on top, cover with Clingfilm or foil and refrigerate until ready to leave for the picnic. As this has a mayonnaise-based sauce, it should really be transported in a cool-box if the weather is likely to be hot.

Salad of cherry tomatoes, baby corn and mange-tout

8 oz (225 g) cherry tomatoes

8 oz (225 g) fresh mange-tout

8 oz (225 g) baby sweet corn

Vinaigrette

¼ pt (150 ml) good (not necessarily best) olive oil

1 tbsp champagne vinegar

salt and pepper to taste

Garnish

chives

Wash the tomatoes but don't peel them. Top and tail the mange-tout and blanch them and the baby corn in boiling salted water for four minutes. Drain immediately under cold running water, and pat dry with kitchen paper.

In a large bowl mix all the ingredients for the vinaigrette. Add the vegetables and mix round gently. Put them in the container in which they will be served, sprinkle with chives, cover and refrigerate.

Note If you don't have very far to travel to your picnic and consequently don't need to keep the Steak Tartare in a cool-box, this salad looks spectacular served from a large round dish surrounding the steak.

Pecan and orange mousse gâteau

This is an absolutely wonderful, rich but light nut cake. Light because it has no flour in it, rich because of all the eggs and the cream in the middle. It is the sort of cake that ends up on the plate looking rather abandoned, so if in transit it loses its pristine neatness – not to worry.

6 oz (175 g) fresh pecan nuts

1 dsp flour

6 eggs

rind from 2 small or 1 large orange

pinch of salt

½ tsp crème of tartar

4 oz (110 g) caster sugar plus 2 tbsp

¼ pt (150 ml) double or whipping cream

Cointreau, Grand Marnier or similar

Heat the oven to 350°F(180°C)Reg 4. Grease and flour two 8 in (20 cm) sandwich tins. Place the pecans on a baking tray and bake for about 5 minutes until warm and lightly roasted. Remove, toss with the flour and grind in a liquidizer or processor. Separate the eggs and beat the yolks with the sugar until thickened and running in ribbons. Grate the orange rind and add to the egg yolks. In a large bowl whisk the egg whites together with the salt and crème of tartar until they stand in soft peaks, add the remaining sugar and beat again. Gently pour the egg yolk mixture over the whites, add about a quarter of the nuts and carefully start to fold in, go on adding the rest of the nut mixture until all the mixture is folded together. Pour into the sandwich tins and place in the middle of the oven at 300°F (150°C) Reg 2 for 45 minutes or until a skewer comes out clean when inserted. Cool in the tins.

When you are ready to assemble the food for the picnic, take the cakes out of the tins and sandwich them together with whipped cream into which you have put a dash of Cointreau or some other orange-based liqueur. Sprinkle icing sugar on top and place either in a cake tin, or plastic cake box or on a plate with two layers of tin foil carefully placed over the cake and tucked in. Put in the car at the last moment if you can't fit it into a cool-box.

AN INDIAN PICNIC

Glyndebourne and India do not immediately appear to have anything in common at all. Neither 'The Pearl Fishers' nor an Indian raga has ever been heard in the opera house and, unlike China, India hasn't embraced the Western operatic tradition. Perhaps years of amateur operatic performances in the days of the Raj with the General's generously proportioned lady singing Mimi, reinforced the Indian people's preference for their own brand of silky sinewy music.

Picnics and India, on the other hand, are well documented. British Army officers went to great lengths (even to the point of writing books and having special picnic baskets made) to make sure that their game pie, cold plum pudding and champagne remained cool and flyless on long journeys in the hot country. But one never hears of the essential beauty and fragrance of Indian food in these picnics. Where are the cool creams and greens of a raita, the flame colours of a tandoori grilled chicken? Surely no-one is suggesting cold plum pudding on the Glydebourne lawn?

With due respect to the gallant officers – no. But it is difficult to find authentic Indian recipes for cold food. It seems that when an Indian party eats outside it is usually for a barbecue of delectably marinated meats. We never do discover what Dr Aziz had brought on his elephant for the picnic at the Marabar Caves in *A Passage to India* apart, that is, from regular supplies of poached eggs and tea. Disaster struck before lunch.

So why include an Indian picnic in the book, so far removed as it is from the misty Englishness of Glyndebourne? Simply because Indian food is delicious and its influence on Western food is growing all the time. Wonderful spices like ginger are now commonplace together with such delicacies as okra and fresh leaf coriander.

As I am not suggesting you take along your barbecue to tandoori the king prawns, this picnic is influenced by, rather than a genuine reproduction of, a cold Indian meal – but is none the less delicious for that.

Mushroom Samosas

Grilled Spiced Chicken Strips with Fresh Tomato Chutney

Cucumber Salad with Yoghurt and Mint

Saffron Rice with Roasted Cashews and Sultanas

Mushroom samosas

Samosas are now found everywhere, not just in supermarkets but in hundreds of Indian and Pakistani-run corner shops which stay open late and provide the perfect midnight snacks. Samosas come in all sorts of different sizes – the more authentic home-made ones seem to be bigger and bear a greater resemblance to the Cornish Pastie than the smaller more uniform mass-produced ones.

Because I don't think people will wish to start a Glyndebourne picnic with a large pastie I have made these smaller and have cut down considerably on the potato to be found in more authentic recipes.

Dough

12 oz (350 g) white unbleached all-purpose flour

salt

4 oz (110 g) softened butter

water

Sift the flour and salt into a bowl, add the butter and rub into the flour until it resembles fine breadcrumbs. Add enough water to form the dough into a ball (about 5 tbsp should be right). Turn onto a lightly floured board and knead for at least 5 minutes. You can, of course, make the dough in a food processor if you prefer. Wrap the ball in a plastic bag and put in the fridge for at least an hour to rest.

Filling

12 oz (350 g) mushrooms

4 cloves garlic, crushed

1 in (2.5 cm) cube fresh ginger, finely grated

1 tbsp yoghurt

3 tbsp sunflower oil

½ tsp salt

1 medium onion, finely chopped

½ tsp turmeric

½ tsp ground cumin

⅛ tsp cayenne (more or less to taste)

4 oz (110 g) frozen petit pois

3 oz (75 g) potato, cut into ¼ in (6 mm) dice

Wipe the mushrooms and chop them roughly, but not too small. Blend the garlic and ginger together in a small cup with the yoghurt and 2 tbsp water.

Heat the oil in a heavy-bottomed pan and add the onion. Fry for several minutes, or until it turns golden brown. Add the turmeric, cumin and cayenne, stir round, then add the garlic and ginger mixture. Let that cook a little and then add the mushrooms, peas and potatoes plus salt to taste. Pour in ¼ pt (150 ml) water, cover and simmer until the water has evaporated and the vegetables are cooked. Stir occasionally to make sure it doesn't burn – you may have to add more water, but the mixture should end up moist with no excess liquid. Set aside to cool.

Remove the dough from the fridge, knead again for a few minutes and divide it into 12 equal balls. On a floured board roll out each ball into a circle of 4 in (10 cm) diameter. Cut the circle in half, then fold each semi-circle in half. Make a cone shape of each semi-circle by sticking the two cut straight edges together with the help of water. Put 1 tbsp of the filling into the cone and fold over and stick the top to form a triangular package. Repeat this process with all of them, making sure all the edges are well sealed.

Heat enough vegetable oil in a deep pan just to cover the samosas. When fairly hot (not as hot as for chips) put them in a single layer and cook gently until golden brown, turning once in the process. Drain well on kitchen paper.

Serve the samosas out of a basket lined with a fresh cloth. They should not be kept in a fridge or cool-box as they are at their best served at room, or warm outdoor temperature. They may be made in advance, in which case reheat them to crisp them up before leaving for the picnic.

Grilled spiced chicken strips

These delicious spicy 'fingers' of chicken have two great advantages for a picnic: they can be eaten in the fingers (or at the very least with a fork) and, most important for Glyndebourne, they can sit in a picnic basket in the boot of the car during the first act without spoiling.

1½ lb (700 g) chicken breasts, boned and skinned

8 cloves garlic, peeled

2 tsp fennel seeds

1 piece fresh ginger (1 in/2.5 cm cube)

3 tsp ground cumin

3 tsp ground coriander

1 tsp ground cardomom

1 tsp ground cinnamon

½ tsp ground cloves

1 tsp salt

1 tbsp tomato purée

3 tbsp red wine vinegar

4 tbsp sunflower oil

Cut the chicken breasts into thin strips about ½ in (1.2 cm) wide and 2–3 in (5–8 cm) long and put them into a bowl. Now put all the other ingredients into a liquidizer and whizz them up to a smooth paste. Mix this with the chicken, making sure all the pieces are well coated with the marinade. Cover and put in a cool place or the fridge for at least 4 hours.

When you are ready to cook them pre-heat the grill and lay the chicken pieces (with the marinade clinging to them) on the grill pan side by side in a single layer. Grill for about 8 minutes on one side and about 5 minutes on the other or until cooked and the marinade has almost burned in patches (the exact time depends very much on the efficiency of your grill). Remove to cool on kitchen paper and cook a second batch if necessary. To serve, place them on a bed of crispy small lettuce leaves (preferably Little Gem) in a shallow dish. Decorate with fresh coriander leaves. Cover with foil and place in the larder or fridge until ready to pack into the picnic basket.

Fresh tomato chutney

This dish is somewhere between a salad and a fresh chutney.

1 lb (450 g) fresh, ripe tomatoes

1 small onion

2 cloves garlic

2 tbsp lemon juice

½ tsp ground coriander

½ tsp ground cumin

1 tsp caster sugar

salt

1 tbsp fresh chopped coriander leaves

1 tsp whole black mustard seeds

2 tbsp vegetable oil

Peel the tomatoes and roughly chop them. Put all the other ingredients except the mustard seeds and oil in the liquidizer or food processor and whizz until the onion is finely chopped and then pour onto the tomatoes and mix thoroughly.

Heat the oil in a very heavy-bottomed small frying pan and when smoking put in the mustard seeds. Wait a few seconds and the seeds will begin to pop, then pour the contents of the pan, oil and all onto the tomatoes. Mix thoroughly and carefully.

Put into a bowl or jar, cover and refrigerate until the time comes to pack up the picnic. Take the chopped coriander separately and sprinkle on just before serving.

Cucumber salad with yoghurt and mint

This is similar to cucumber raita which often accompanies tandoori dishes, except that the cucumber is sliced not grated, and mint is added.

1 small or ½ large cucumber

1 × 5 oz (150 g) carton yoghurt

black pepper, freshly ground

1 tbsp mint, freshly chopped

salt

Peel the cucumber and slice it thinly. Pour the yoghurt into a bowl and mix until smooth. Add the cucumber, black pepper and mint (but not the salt) and mix carefully but thoroughly. Put in the fridge until ready to pack for the picnic.

It is advisable to take the salt separately and add it just before you eat otherwise it will make the cucumber 'weep' and when you get it to the picnic it will be very watery.

Mint is also a little temperamental as it very soon discolours or shrivels up when chopped and put on food. If you mix it well into the cucumber it will impart its flavour and the appearance won't matter. Take a separate sprig of mint to chop over the cucumber at the last minute if you wish.

Saffron rice with roasted cashews and sultanas

Without doubt one of the world's great culinary mysteries is leaf saffron – the dried stigma of the wild crocus. You may find it in shrivelled, heaped abundance in markets in Greece, Spain or the Far East or locked away behind glass in tiny phials in smart delicatessens in New York not to be touched until the manager of the store importantly finds his keys. But wherever you are it is like gold dust – it looks like gold-dust and it is almost as expensive. But why the fuss? What is so special about saffron? There are, after all, other ways of turning food yellow by using turmeric, or yellow food colouring. The answer is that no other ingredient has the evocative fragrance and subtle taste that real saffron brings to a dish along with its beauty.

This rice dish can be cooked with turmeric instead of saffron and makes a delicious and attractive alternative, but quite simply you get what you pay for.

I have found through long experience of making rice salads that a firm long-grained rice such as Uncle Ben's is the most satisfactory. Bismati rice is essential when cooking a hot Indian meal but is not very reliable when it comes to cooling down and sitting about.

¾ tsp saffron *or* ½ tsp turmeric

2 tbsp warm milk

sunflower oil

1 stick cinnamon

4 cardomom pods

8 oz (225 g) long-grained rice

1 tsp salt

2 tbsp sunflower oil

2 oz (50 g) unsalted cashew nuts

3 oz (75 g) sultanas

2 tbsp light vinaigrette dressing (see page 101)

Dry-roast the saffron by putting it in a small heavy-bottomed frying pan or skillet over a low flame. Push the leaves about until they are a dark reddish colour. Crumble them into the warm milk and leave for a couple of hours.

Heat the oil in a saucepan and add the cinnamon and cardomom, stir until they begin to darken and add the rice. Stir again and add water according to the instructions on the packet and 1 tsp salt. Cover and cook over a low heat for half the cooking time (probably 10 minutes). Stir round with a fork and add the saffron and milk. Stir again, cover and leave until completely cooked (another 10 minutes). When cooked, tip the rice into a sieve, take out the whole spices and run cold water through it. Leave to cool.

Heat 2 tbsp sunflower oil in a heavy pan and add the cashew

nuts. Turning them round all the time, wait for them to turn a uniform golden brown all over. Remove onto kitchen paper to drain.

If you are going to use turmeric instead of the saffron simply put it into the pan with the rice before you add the water. Stir round and proceed as above.

Put the rice in a white china dish, add the sultanas and the light vinaigrette, mix thoroughly and sprinkle the cashews over the top. Put in the fridge until ready to pack up for the picnic.

Madhur Jaffry, whose marvellous television series provided the inspiration for many people to try Indian cookery, says in one of her books, 'In Europe and America, most meals end with dessert and coffee, in India most meals end with fruit . . .' I shall take her at her experienced word. There are, of course, wonderful Indian desserts, very sweet and not altogether suitable for a summer picnic of limited duration.

My suggestion, therefore, is that you take a selection of rather exotic fruits, knives and forks to prepare and eat them with, and large napkins.

Alternatively you could make an exotic fruit salad with lychees, melon and mangoes. Squeeze some lemon juice over it and serve without cream.

A ROMANTIC PICNIC

There can be few more Romantic places on earth than Glyndebourne. Picture the gardens: great noble trees, water-lillied lake surrounded by smooth grass paths mown from meadows of cow parsley, marguerites and naturalised tulips. The Downs, sculptured by moving clouds and the soft gauzy green light of an English summer evening are in the distance. It is a setting which many a Romantic novelist would have been proud to invent.

At the risk of gilding the lily, add to that the food of love itself – music – and music in its most romantic form – opera. Night after night in the opera house undying love is sworn: Alfredo to Violetta, Rodolfo to Mimi, Octavian to Sophie and eight hundred hearts swell as they remember what was, or is, or perhaps will be.

So, if music be the food of love, who needs a picnic? Certainly lovers do, for love creates a prodigious appetite, despite the erroneous myth that the only sustenance a man needs is to feast upon Araminta's eyes; unfortunately the goodies to be found there will not satisfy an unromantically rumbling stomach. The goodies to be found in this picnic will.

It is, of course, for two; a simple uncomplicated affair to be eaten off a rug in the long grass in the wild garden or in seclusion by one of the lower lakes. There will be none of the tiresome complications of middle-age – the inability to heave yourself off the ground once established there, the insistence on three different wines, little pots of this and that, bottles, boxes, cloths, furniture. Just each other, some pink champagne, a Coeur à la Crème and perhaps a hint of passion fruit. And, after the performance, a walk around the lake hand in hand, and a Baccio (one of those delectable Italian chocolates, each with a lovers' motto).

Tartelettes with Crab and Prawns

Galantine of Poussin and Quail with Mushroom, Fennel and Walnut Stuffing

Salad of Cherry Tomatoes and Avocados

Potato Salad with Walnuts and Dill

Coeur à la Crème with Passion Fruit Sauce

Tartelettes with crab and prawns

These attractive little tarts can be eaten in the fingers and are made from ingredients known since ancient times for their aphrodisiac qualities: seafood. (Although our romantic picnickers are likely to blanch at such lack of subtlety.)

This quantity will make about 24 tiny tarts, too many for one sitting but they will keep in the fridge. The pastry is very short and light so it is important to pack them very carefully.

Pastry

2 oz (50 g) cooking fat (half butter, half blended fat or lard)

4 oz (110 g) white flour (or half white and half brown)

1 small egg yolk

water

Rub the fat into the flour. Add half the egg yolk and enough water to make a firmish dough (about 1 dsp). Form into a ball, wrap in plastic or foil and put in the fridge to rest for at least half an hour.

Turn out on to a floured board and roll out to ¼ in (6 mm) thick. Cut into rounds and place in patty pans, if possible the very small, cocktail variety. Into each pan put some greaseproof paper and a few dried beans. Bake blind in a hot oven (425°F/220°C/Reg 7) for 10 minutes. Remove the paper and beans and cook again for a couple more minutes until completely dried out. Remove and cool on a rack.

Filling

2 oz (50 g) soft cream cheese

1½ tbsp mayonnaise

½ tsp curry powder

squeeze lemon juice

1 clove garlic, crushed

3 oz (75 g) white crab meat

2 oz (50 g) prawns

salt and pepper

paprika for decoration

Put the cheese into a bowl and soften with a fork. Add the mayonnaise, curry powder, lemon juice and garlic and mix thoroughly until blended and smooth. Break the crab meat into it and add the roughly chopped prawns. Mix together gently. Add salt and pepper to taste and put into the fridge. When the time comes to pack up for the picnic, spoon the fish mixture into the pastry cases, sprinkle a little paprika on top and place side by side into a dish which is slightly deeper than the tarts themselves. Cover with foil and put into the picnic basket.

Galantine of poussin and quail with mushroom, fennel and walnut stuffing

This is a charming dish. You slice the little poussin in half and the different layers of texture and colour are miraculously revealed. Don't be daunted by the prospect of boning the birds. There are three essentials for the task – a *very* sharp pointed knife, a lot of uninterrupted time, and patience. If you are without any of these three ask your nearest special butcher or friendly restaurant to do it for you.

1 petit poussin

1 quail

salt and pepper

2 small bulbs fennel

juice of ½ lemon

Stuffing

6 oz (175 g) flat mushrooms

1 oz (25 g) butter

salt and pepper

fennel (see method)

2 oz (50 g) chopped walnuts

1 oz (25 g) soft brown breadcrumbs

1 small egg

dill for decoration

First bone the two birds. Lay them out flat and rub them with a little salt and pepper. Clean the fennel, taking off the very hard outer layer, and poach it in lightly salted water to which you have added the lemon juice until just cooked (about 5 minutes depending on the size of the bulbs). Drain the fennel and take them apart until you reveal the hearts. One of them you will need to keep whole to put into the centre of the quail so choose whichever fits the best. The other one, together with the rest of the cooked fennel, will go into the stuffing.

To make the stuffing, wipe the mushrooms and slice them. Melt the butter in a frying pan and add the mushrooms. Sprinkle with salt and pepper and cook until soft and the excess liquid has been absorbed. Put the mushrooms, fennel (excluding the heart you have retained for stuffing the quail) and walnuts into a food processor and blend in short bursts until chopped (but *not* pulverized). Turn into a basin and add the breadcrumbs and enough beaten egg to bind it. If you prefer a looser stuffing, omit the egg. Add seasoning to taste.

Now spread the poussin, which you have flat on a board, with the stuffing – you may not need all of it, it entirely depends on how big your poussin is. The stuffing should be about ½ in (1.2 cm) thick. Onto the stuffing put the quail and onto the quail the reserved fennel heart. Now very carefully wrap the quail round the fennel and then the poussin and stuffing round the quail. It is much simpler than it sounds as the ingredients will be amenable to being pushed around into any shape you wish. You just must make sure that the stuffing surrounds the quail. Here it is important to stress that if you have over-stuffed the bird it is very likely to split whilst cooking. Make sure therefore that you have a comfortable amount of stuffing in it, and gently mould the poussin into a bird shape. Sew the flaps at the back of the poussin together with a large needle and tough cotton (it will be removed after cooking so don't worry about the neatness of your stitches!) making sure that all the cracks are sewn together. Gently place the bird, which should look like a rather flattened little chicken, in a baking dish. Rub with salt and pepper and a little butter and roast in a medium oven (400°F/200°C/Reg 6) for 30 minutes. Turn the oven down to 350°F(180°C)Reg 4 and cook for a further 30 minutes. When cooked, gently lift out and leave to get quite cold.

To prepare for the picnic. Turn the poussin onto its tummy and carefully take out all the stitches. Place the right way up on a bed of fresh crisp lettuce leaves and decorate with dill or fennel leaves, cover and pack into your picnic basket. This dish should be served with a mayonnaise made with walnut oil. If you decide not to make the potato salad in the recipe below, make and take the mayonnaise separately to eat with the poussin.

Salad of cherry tomatoes and avocados

8 oz (225 g) cherry tomatoes

1 small avocado

juice of 1 lemon

2 tbsp good-quality olive oil

salt and pepper

Wash the tomatoes, cut in half and put in a bowl. Peel and slice the avocados in long slices and put them straight into a bowl with the lemon juice. Mix them around gently, making sure that they are completely covered in the juice to avoid discoloration. Transfer them to the bowl with the tomatoes. Pour over the olive oil and add salt and pepper to taste. Cover and refrigerate until ready to pack for the picnic.

Potato salad with walnuts and dill

This really delicious potato salad is the recipe of Craig Ruttenberg, who worked for many years at Glyndebourne as a distinguished member of the Music Staff.

1 lb (450 g) new potatoes

½ pt (275 ml) mayonnaise flavoured with 2 tbsp walnut oil, sunflower oil and a couple of shakes of Worcestershire sauce

2 tbsp chopped walnuts

1 tbsp chopped dill

Clean the potatoes well but don't peel or scrape them unless you must. Boil them in salted water until just tender. Drain and set aside to cool.

Make the mayonnaise using the walnut oil in conjunction with sunflower or a light olive oil and add a shake or two of Worcestershire sauce at the end.

Slice the potatoes and combine them with the mayonnaise, walnuts and chopped dill.

Coeur à la crème with passion fruit sauce

These little heart-shaped puddings are exquisite – simple classic French food at its best. You will need the special dishes to make them in, however: small heart-shaped cocottes with holes in the bottom to allow the mixture to drain. They can be bought from specialist kitchen shops. This quantity will make enough for 3 people but making less is hardly worth it.

½ pt (275 ml) fresh double cream

2 egg whites

Whip the cream until it is stiff. Beat the egg whites until they form soft peaks and fold into the cream. Line your heart-shaped mould or moulds with clean muslin and spoon the mixture into it. Wrap the muslin over the top and leave, standing on a plate in a cool place until the next day when the cream will have drained. Take plates with you to the picnic to turn the hearts out on to and pour over the Passion Fruit Sauce.

Sauce

6 ripe passion fruits (choose crinkled ones, they are riper)

3 oz (75 g) caster sugar

1 tsp arrowroot or cornflour

Cut the tops off the passion fruit and scoop all the flesh out into a small pan. Add the sugar and stir on a low flame until thoroughly heated through but not boiling. This helps with the next step. Pour the pulp into a sieve and force all the juice and flesh through, leaving the little black seeds behind. You will now have a wonderful golden-coloured juice. Dissolve the arrowroot in a little water, add to the passion fruit and pour back into the pan. Stir until it boils, thickens and becomes clear. Take it off the heat and allow to cool. Pour into a plastic pot with a lid to take to the picnic.

A PERSONAL CHOICE

I first went to Glyndebourne in 1955 with Anthony and Val Goldthorp. The opera was Rossini's 'Le Comte d'Ory': my eyes were opened. Goldthorp was then a director (later the Chairman) of O.W. Loeb & Co. Ltd, the well-known German wine shippers, in London's Adelphi. The principal, Dr Otto Loeb – a refugee from Germany in the Thirties – was founder of the firm and a friend of the late John Christie, sharing his love of excellence in food, wine and music. Loeb's delicious wines from the Mosel and Rhine were to have an established, if not dominant, place on the 'Wallop' lists until Moran Caplat's retirement a few years ago.

The luxury of this trip to Glyndebourne with the Goldthorps was to continue for many years, eagerly anticipated by Elisabeth, my wife, and me as we packed our glad rags in our Yorkshire home and headed south for four days of unadulterated bliss. Our hosts, however, always used the restaurants and never picnicked (to my relief, I have to add).

Much of my humble musical knowledge was gained from Anthony Goldthorp; certainly my personal repertoire was built from hearing first performances of eclectic operas and, of course, from listening to the entire Mozart *oeuvre*, though it was many years before I was to enjoy 'La Clemenza di Tito', and that was not at Glyndebourne.

Meanwhile, Sir John Pritchard had become a close friend. In those far-off days he was conductor of the Royal Liverpool Philharmonic Orchestra and busy with *Musica Viva*, as well as being on the music staff at Glyndebourne. He subsequently commenced his long reign as musical director there.

My sojourns with him, at first at his rented house 'Dacres' in Lewes, were memorable for the balmy evenings on the terrace, when I would sit with him sipping an after-performance glass of champagne – always vintage – and imbibing more about opera from the mouth of a master. Later, too, in his lovely Elizabethan home near Hailsham, I would add to the picnic destined for the conductor's room (whenever the redoubtable Mrs Mills, Pritchard's erstwhile housekeeper, would permit me to superimpose her legendary stuffed eggs, cigarette ash and all).

Many are the now-famous singers, producers and

Lobster Bellevue

Terrine de Canard Truffé an Foie Gras

Crisp Chocolate and Lemon and Cream Cheesecake

designers I met, out on the balcony overlooking the inner courtyard (also known as the staff canteen and overseen by a young man known to all as 'Courtyard Richard'). Of the many who spent a season at the opera house and partook with us are such household names as Messel, Montrésor, Cox and Hockney.

Each year I would confect and transport down from the North Pritchard's favourite dish – a luscious Terrine de Canard Truffé au Foie Gras avec son Gelée de Rubis. He liked it largely because of an alternative name one magnificent Glyndebourne benefactor from Yorkshire gave to it following a Musical Evening at Lord Harewood's house, for which I'd prepared many of my specialities – he called it 'Michael's Nice Potted Meat'!

Some time in the late Sixties or early Seventies John together with then Mr George Christie asked me to lunch on a boat moored on the Thames. I remember it well for it had an unforgettable ceiling (if that is what it is called on a boat) lined in shocking-pink felt studded with pea-lights.

'Would I undertake the catering at Glyndebourne?' Sadly, the timing was wrong. Later, Brian Dickie was to ask my advice on whom should be asked to re-style the menus in the audience dining rooms of Middle, Nether and Over Wallop. I gave my opinion but also strongly recommended that whoever they eventually might appoint should institute a buffet – for the entirely selfish reason that it gave people more time to stroll round the gardens. (Did I really influence this excellent move in any way? I hope so.)

The dishes for my personal menu are naturally those served many times on that balcony, overlooking the courtyard.

Lobster Bellevue

1 heaped tsp paprika
1 tbsp oil
1 tbsp white or red wine vinegar
1 small onion, peeled and quartered
12 black peppercorns
1 × 1½– 2 lb (700–900 g) live lobster
Garnish
stiff home-made mayonnaise
hard-boiled egg, quartered
tomato segments, skinned and seeded
cucumber slices
a few prawns
small sprigs of watercress

To boil the lobster, select a pan large enough and deep enough to contain the lobster. Pour in 6 pt (3.5 l) of water, add salt and bring to the boil. Add all ingredients except the lobster and bring to the boil. Reduce the heat and simmer for 10 minutes.

Bring this liquid (called a *court bouillon*) back to the boil and pop in the lobster. Bring back to boiling point and simmer for 15 minutes. Leave the lobster to cool in the liquid for 2 hours. Remove the lobster from the pan and leave to cool covered with a damp clean cloth.

To split or open a cooked lobster, break off the claws where they join the body. Bend back and crack the small pincer at the 'hinge'. With a hammer or rolling pin crack, but do not crush, the main claw sufficiently to allow the removal of the white meat with a lobster pick, fork or bodkin (a small knitting needle is also good for this job). Crack each knuckle likewise.

Open out the tail and lay the lobster flat, the head to the right. You will notice a line running the length of the fish with a 'cross' about 2 in (5 cm) down from the eyes. Plunge the point of a heavy cook's knife right through this cross down to the board. The knife should be vertical at this stage. Now bring the knife down, cutting firmly through the line of the head and ending with the head split in half. Turn the lobster round completely. Open the tail out flat again. Insert the knife at the same point and, in exactly the same way, cut through the line and on to the end of the tail.

Open out the two halves. Remove the 'string' or dark thread (intestine) which should be obvious in the centre of one or other halves of the tail (sometimes it is empty and almost transparent and difficult to see – but you'll find it!). Right at the head end you will see the 'sack' which has a slightly papery appearance. Remove this from both halves with a teaspoon and discard. Leave everything else, including the eggs or coral, the greenish part which some consider to be a delicacy, and any pink and white creamy-looking substance. Leave all the smaller claws as they are.

Remove the crescent of pink and white meat from each tail. Turn this flat-side down on to the board and cut each into 5 or 6 pieces to put back on to the filled or stuffed tail.

The lobster is ready for serving. Simply replace the cut tail meat, put a lemon wedge in the body cavity, lay the cracked claw alongside and serve on a large plate with a bowl of mayonnaise.

For a special occasion you may want to gild the lily. Fill the entire length of each half shell with a fine, small-diced Russian Salad or Potato Salad.

Invert each cut lobster tail on to the *opposite* shell so that the curved coral pink lobster meat is uppermost on the bed of salad. Remove the meat from each cracked claw, keeping it whole if you can. Arrange this on top of the main part of the body, near the head.

Pipe swirls and rosettes of very stiff mayonnaise down the shell. Decorate with quarters of hard-boiled egg, skinned and seeded tomato segments, cucumber twists, a prawn or two and small sprigs of watercress. I often remove the solid coral and press this through a hair sieve, sprinkling a little over the decorated lobster and mixing the remainder into a good tablespoon or two of the

mayonnaise.
Note Bottled mayonnaise is rarely stiff enough to pipe, so if used omit this operation and serve it separately in a sauceboat.

Terrine de canard truffé au foie gras

- **1 × 4–5 lb (1.8–2.3 kg) duck, dressed weight**
- **salt and freshly milled pepper**
- **3 tbsp Madeira or sherry, medium dry**
- **2 tbsp brandy**
- **1 × 1 oz (25 g) tin of truffles (retaining their liquor)**
- **1 small clove garlic, cut in half**
- **1 small bay leaf**
- **1 × 8 oz (225 g) tin pâté de foie gras (or Swiss parfait)**
- **2 lb (900 g) loin of pork**
- **8 oz (225 g) extra pork fat**
- **1 large egg, beaten**
- **1 slightly heaped tsp gelatine crystals**
- **4 oz (110 g) butter, melted**
- **oil**
- **1 lb (450 g) streaky bacon to line the mould**

Cut the breasts and legs off the duck. Take the skin and any bone off the breasts and put these, whole, in a shallow pie dish, seasoning lightly with salt and pepper. Pour over the Madeira and brandy, the juice from the tin of truffles, the garlic and bay leaf. Cover with plastic film and leave to marinate for 4 hours, turning the breasts every hour.

Put the tin of parfait or foie gras in the fridge so that it is set but not frozen.

Strip the meat from the legs and take off any scraps of meat from the duck carcass. Discard any skin (use the carcass and bones for stock for soup). Skin and bone the piece of loin pork and cut this and the fat and duck leg meat into small pieces. Using the metal blade on a food processor make a very fine purée, or put the meats twice through the fine blade of a mincer.

Season lightly and use the beaten egg and marinade to moisten things as you go along. (Discard the bay leaf and garlic.) You must also sprinkle in the dry gelatine crystals at intervals during the purée-ing process. (These crystals are *not* to be dissolved in the usual manner.) Also pour in the cool but melted butter during this process.

Now you are ready to 'build' the terrine. Brush a 4-pound terrine, seamless loaf tin or other suitable deep mould thoroughly with oil or butter and line it with the bacon.

Mentally divide the pork mixture into 4 equal quantities. Have a bowl of cold water to hand. Scoop out one quarter of the mixture and put into the base of the terrine. Dip the fingers into cold water and pat the mixture level with the back of the fingers, pushing it well into the corners, dipping into the water to facilitate the process.

Open the chilled tin of foie gras or parfait at both ends and push the pâté out. Cut the truffles into quarters. Measure the length of your terrine then, depending on the length of the foie gras, cut this into 2 or 3 slices so that you can put one long strip down the centre.

Cut each marinated duck breast in half lengthways and lay two of the pieces end to end on top of the layer of pork mixture already in the terrine. Cover with a portion of the pork purée, again patting well with wetted fingers.

Next lay the foie gras pieces in one long line down the centre, pressing the truffle pieces into it. Cover this with the next portion of purée. Lay on the second breast pieces and cover with the remaining purée, patting and smoothing everything into place. Give the mould a sharp bang on the table top, which will help settle things into place. Fold over the bacon flaps.

Cover with a lid, which should be buttered at the edges, or a piece of buttered foil. Stand the terrine in a roasting tin of hot water coming two-thirds up the sides, and bake on the centre shelf of the oven at 400°F (200°C) Reg 6 for 1¼ hours or until the juices are clear. There will be evidence of pale pink 'scum': this is OK. Take the lid or foil off for the last 20 minutes of the cooking time so that the bacon browns somewhat.

Leave the terrine to cool completely, standing it on a wire cake rack. Now, find a piece of wood which will just fit inside the extremities of the terrine. Cover this with foil. Put a 7 lb (3.2 kg) weight or small stone on top and put into the refrigerator to chill, press and set.

To Unmould
Run a heated palette knife very carefully round the sides of the terrine, taking care not to damage the bacon lining and dipping the knife into boiling water when necessary. Stand the base of the terrine in a sink containing an inch of scalding water for 30 seconds to melt the butter coating.

Then, clear your work top of all its items, lift the terrine and invert it onto the work top with a mighty bang. This should do it! If there is an air lock, slide a rigid knife down the end of the terrine while it is still upside down and press and pull gently but firmly until you hear and feel it release.

Serve the terrine on a starched folded napkin on your most attractive meat dish. Cut into ¼ in (6 mm) slices and eat with a knife and fork.

A delicate crab apple, quince or apple jelly is an excellent accompaniment.
Serves 8–10

Crisp chocolate and lemon and cream cheesecake

6 medium eggs, separated

3 oz (75 g) caster sugar, mixed with

3 oz (75 g) icing sugar, sieved

2 oz (50 g) cocoa powder, sieved

1 tsp vanilla extract

This cake is soft to handle, hence the use of a board for ease of transporting. Pre-heat the oven to 350°F (180°C) Reg 4. Butter, and line with buttered paper as well, a Swiss Roll tin 14 × 9 in (35 × 23 cm) and 1 in (2.5 cm) deep. Cream the yolks with the two sugars and the vanilla until thick and ribboning.

Using a balloon whisk, cut and mix in the cocoa powder thoroughly. Beat the egg white to a soft peak (you don't want a 'dry' meringue, but stiffish). Cut and mix well in half the egg whites. Cut and fold in the remainder. There shouldn't be any fluffy bits, but don't over-work the mixture. Pour the mixture into the tin and bake in the centre of the oven for 25 minutes or until springy to the touch.

Cool completely before turning the cake out and removing the paper. Have ready a square cake-board or a flat platter 9 × 9 in (23 × 23 cm).

Filling and topping

1 × 8 oz (225 g) bar of dessert chocolate

4 oz (110 g) Philadelphia cream cheese

1 heaped tbsp icing sugar, sieved

strained juice of 1 lemon

icing sugar for dredging

Break the chocolate into its squares and put in a glass bowl over a pan of just simmering water (or melt it in a microwave). As soon as it is softened, remove the basin, beat the chocolate smooth with a spoon, and spread it over the entire oblong cake. Cut the cake in half and carefully lift one half onto the board or platter.

Beat the cream cheese, icing sugar and enough of the juice to give a good lemony flavour (if the lemon is very large, there might be too much juice). Spread this over the cake and sit the top on. Put the cake in the fridge to set the chocolate. Dredge with a good coating of icing sugar.
Serves 8

PACKING AND WRAPPING

Boiling water / heating liquids Many of the grander cars have an electrical point where you can plug in a travelling kettle. Small Butane or Propane gas burners are best for heating or boiling, but you will be well advised to take along an old tray on which to stand such a burner for safety.

You might also take along a sheet of heavy duty card, suitably scored, for bending, and covered with foil, to act as a windshield. Ensure the pan 'grid' is large enough to hold your utensil safely.

Containers Square containers are easier to pack than round ones. Take your cool box along to the shop and experiment with different sizes which will fit economically into your box or boxes.

Have 4 pieces of wood, or heavy-duty cardboard tube. Cut ½ in (1.2 cm) longer than the highest container you will usually be packing. These stand in the 4 corners of your cool-box to support a shelf of perspex which should be cut to fit especially for this job.

Decanters Stoppers should be Sellotaped down (and round). Choose a box just large enough to contain the decanter standing upright. Pack round tightly with bubble-wrap or newspaper. Fit the box into a deep carrier bag for ease of carrying.

Dry ice If you can readily obtain this, then it is very efficacious. *BUT – BE WARNED!* Dry ice can burn you severely, so use a leather glove or an oven glove when handling (not plastic or rubber gloves as these will stick to dry ice) and pack the ice in those special foil-type bags, not directly on top of the containers. Keep container and cool-box lids shut at all times.

Glass Each glass should be wrapped in bubble-wrap.

Ice for cooling Remember that 1 'jelly' or freezer pack won't do much good. The average cool-box needs at least 4. Cool the box itself before packing, either by standing it in your fridge if it's big enough, or by running cold water into it for 10 minutes.

Ice for drinks This is packed in a Thermos container. Remember to take ice-tongs!

Mayonnaise, Cream and Sauces Transport these separately, in air-tight lidded containers.

Place Settings Individual place settings can be wrapped in the napkin and held with a rubber band. Groups of settings should then be placed into a plastic bag to prevent wayward pieces of cutlery from dropping out, and to keep the napkin clean.

Salts and peppers If you are taking your best salts, then carry the salt itself in a separate little container to fill on site.

Seating and ground protection Refer to Michael Smith's *Handbook for Hosts* (chapter on 'Picnics').

Tarts and pastries To wrap any fragile tart or pastry, make a loose-ish collar of tissue paper – not greaseproof as this isn't flexible enough – curl this round your fingers to a size which will fit around the item to be packed snugly. Pinch to hold. If the food is moist, such as a stuffed half-egg, roll up a piece of plastic film with the tissue paper. Clip or staple together.

Pack items in one layer, scrunching more pieces of tissue to prevent things sliding about. Make a flat cushion of paper to wedge between the top of the items and the lid of the container.

Put on a sticker marked 'This Way Up' or 'Do Not Tilt'.

Line all plastic boxes with a sheet of greaseproof paper. This will absorb oils and wayward fillings and prevents any possible odours from the plastic transferring to the fresh food. Pernickerty, but probably worth while.

Thermos containers These should be chilled, (or heated, whichever is appropriate, before filling. The flasks should be packed and wedged upright in boxes or baskets for ease of transporting.

EXTRAS AND EMERGENCIES

The ardent *fête champêtriste* will make his or her picnicking life easier by heeding the following advice.

Coping with the dirty china
Take along this special kit:
1 roll of really absorbent kitchen paper (some isn't so absorbent which doesn't help when dealing with mayonnaise) for wiping plates.
1 plastic bag to hold the used dirty papers.
1 plastic bag for bits and bones on the plates.

Drinks Hamper If you are taking a lot of cold wine (champagne, wine for the main course and maybe a pudding wine), buy a bag of crushed ice or ice cubes and pack the bottles flat, with layers of ice, in a cool-box. The ice will probably melt, depending on how far and for how long you travel, but it is a simple matter to pour away the water. The bottles can be disposed of in the nearest litter bin, or brought back home to be disposed of in your own bottle bank or dustbin.
Red wines can be decanted at home into sherry decanters – the flattish-bowled variety – or into broad, flat-bottomed ship's decanters. Transport these in cardboard boxes packed round with crumpled newspapers, their stoppers securely taped.
Alternatively transport the wine in bottles in a partitioned wine box together with corkscrews, openers, etc.

Emergencies A First Aid kit should be in every car. In addition, the birds and bees and other beasties are at large in the gardens and enjoying themselves enormously as they watch you from their perches up in the trees or swoop around overhead with ne'er a thought where they might next spend a penny (or whatever). So, a bottle of Dab-It-Off or some such cleaning fluid or a damp cloth should be to hand in a plastic bag. Wasps will perhaps take a liking to your honeyed salad dressing, and whilst the sturdy member of the party will assure you that 'they won't hurt you' – probably they won't, and hopefully. But – you might just be at the mercy of an insect that is feeling out-of-sorts and decides to get you. So take along: Fly swat, Insect repellent, Wasp-eeze.

Red wine spills NOT SALT – salt fixes the dye. A neutralizing splash of white wine or soda water is best, if done quickly.

And finally GLYNDEBOURNE PICNICKERS DO NOT LEAVE LITTER. Not even the top of the mayonnaise tube.

Anchovy butter

12 oz (350 g) unsalted butter, softened

2 cloves of garlic, crushed

24 anchovy fillets (tinned variety)

2 tsp lemon juice

tip of a tsp cayenne *or* 6–8 drops of Tabasco

½ tsp freshly ground black pepper

In a liquidiser , make a purée of all the ingredients, then rub the mixture through a fine-meshed sieve.
Note There is no added salt in this recipe.

Basil butter

12 oz (350 g) unsalted butter, softened

1 tbsp tomato purée

1 tsp lemon juice

1 tsp caster sugar

1 tsp salt

1 packed teacup basil leaves, freshly picked and rinsed

Make a fine purée of the first five ingredients, adding the basil leaves towards the end so that some texture is left.

Chive butter

12 oz (350 g) unsalted butter, softened

ground white pepper

1 tsp lemon juice

1 teacup chives, very finely snipped

Beat the butter with the pepper and lemon juice. Mix in the snipped chives.

Foie gras and artichoke butter

6 oz (175 g) unsalted butter, softened

1 × 4 oz (110 g) tin of Mousse de Foie Gras *or* Parfait de Foie Gras

1 scant tsp salt

freshly ground white pepper

6 tsp orange juice

1x 4 oz (110 g) tin artichoke bottoms, drained, rinsed and drained again

Chop the artichoke bottoms very finely. In a liquidizer, make a fine purée of the remaining ingredients. Scrape them into a bowl and mix in the chopped artichoke.

Garlic butter

8 large cloves of garlic, peeled

12 oz (350 g) unsalted butter, softened

1 tsp salt

2 tsp lemon juice

For sandwiches, the garlic aroma must be soft and gentle. So, blanch the garlic in boiling water for 2 minutes. Drain and cool. Push through a garlic press and beat into the softened butter along with the salt and lemon juice.

Horseradish butter

12 oz (350 g) unsalted butter, softened

2 tbsp freshly scraped horseradish root, finely grated

2 tsp lemon juice

2 tsp caster sugar

1 tsp salt

In a liquidizer, make a fine purée of all the ingredients.

Lemon butter

12 oz (350 g) unsalted butter, softened

1 tsp salt

ground white pepper

juice and finely grated zest of 1 lemon

Make a paste of all the ingredients in a liquidizer. Rub through a fine-meshed sieve.

Lemon and parsley butter

Make up one batch of Lemon Butter as above. After sieving, add 1 teacup of very finely chopped, freshly picked parsley.

Mint butter

12 oz (350 g) unsalted butter, softened

20–24 large mint leaves, picked and rinsed

2 tsp lemon juice

1 tsp salt

1 tsp sugar

Make a fine purée of all the ingredients in a liquidizer. Rub through a fine-meshed sieve.

Mixed herb butter

12 oz (350 g) unsalted butter, softened

4 tbsp each of parsley; fennel fronds; chervil and chives *or* basil *or* tarragon; chives and flat-leaf parsley

½ clove garlic, crushed

1 tsp lemon juice

1 tsp salt

freshly ground pepper to taste

Finely chop the herbs and blend together all the ingredients.

Mustard butter

12 oz (350 g) unsalted butter, softened

2 tbsp mild French mustard

1 tbsp lemon juice

Beat everything to a smooth paste.

Tarragon butter

12 oz (350 g) unsalted butter, softened

1 packed teacup French tarragon leaves, freshly picked and rinsed

1 tbsp tarragon vinegar, warmed

1 tsp salt

freshly ground pepper

In a liquidizer make a fine purée of the ingredients. (The vinegar is warmed to help it emulsify in cold weather.) Rub through a fine-meshed sieve.

Tomato butter

12 oz (350 g) unsalted butter, softened

2 tbsp tomato purée

½ tsp ground mace *or* dried rosemary *or* nutmeg

1 tsp brown sugar

1 tsp salt

¼ tsp freshly ground black pepper

1 tbsp dry sherry, warmed in cold weather

Make a fine purée of all the ingredients.

Tomato curry and orange butter

12 oz (350 g) unsalted butter, softened

1 tsp salt

2 tbsp good tomato purée

1 tsp finely grated orange zest

1 heaped tsp mild Madras curry powder or paste

Mix all the ingredients together in a liquidiser. Rub through a fine-meshed sieve and put them into wax or plastic cartons. Chill until required in either the freezer or the refrigerator. When ready to use, take the butter out of the freezer or refrigerator and allow it to come to room temperature.

Watercress butter

4 bunches crisp dark-leaf watercress

10 oz (275 g) unsalted butter, softened

1 tsp caster sugar

1 tsp salt

Pick all the leaves from the watercress and discard the stalks. Drop the leaves into a pan of lightly salted boiling water for 30 seconds only. Drain, rinse under cold water and drain again. Squeeze out excess water. In a liquidizer, make a purée of the leaves, the softened butter, the sugar and salt.

INDEX